The Doctrines of
GRACE

In this book, *The Doctrines of Grace*, Roger Skepple has done a remarkable job. He clearly presents unchanging words to an ever-changing world. The truths he presents are seldom proclaimed, often misunderstood, frequently misrepresented and greatly needed. His presentation is accomplished in a comprehensive and thorough manner of the subjects at hand. He not only makes it clear for understanding but also clear that there is no misunderstanding. This book will help its reader to come to grips with what is wrong with man by nature, and what is glorious about God in His redemptive work in salvation.

–Keelan A. Atkinson, Pastor/Teacher
Word Fellowship Reformed Baptist Church

This book is about the doctrines of grace, biblical teaching about the sovereignty of God at work in our salvation. The doctrines of grace offer a perspective on salvation in which God truly is God, so that everything depends on His will and works to His glory. The doctrines of grace and the sovereignty of God are joy-giving, life-changing, Christ-exalting, God-glorifying, missions-motivating, evangelism-encouraging, and discipleship-promoting truth. If you think the teaching of God's sovereignty in sinners' salvation is a man-made idea, you'll think again after you have read this wonderful book. Roger Skepple clearly and comprehensively lays the groundwork for the doctrines of grace. Because of Roger's exegetical skill I seek to devour whatever he writes. I highly recommend it!

–Eddie D. Jacks, Pastor
Resurrected Baptist Church

The most important subject in the world deserves fresh voices and improved clarity in every generation. Pastor Roger Skepple Sr. has given us just that in this treatment of Reformed soteriology. He does not attempt, in this work, to present novel and creative adaptations and innovations concerning this doctrine. Orthodoxy has been preserved and proclaimed with pastoral charity and pedagogical lucidity.

–Hensworth W. C. Jonas, Presiding Elder, East Caribbean Baptist Mission (Antigua & Barbuda)

Pastor Skepple has not shrunken back from presenting the whole counsel of God on this subject to his readers. I thank and praise God for gifting Pastor Skepple with the ability to communicate high and lofty theological truths in such a clear, concise, correct, and readable way. In his book, *The Doctrines of Grace*, Pastor Skepple's theological scholarship shines through and he has held tenaciously to related biblical truths. Yet he has done so in such a compassionate way, that his love, care, and concern for the readers of his book emanates from its pages in such a way that even Christians who disagree with his conclusions will appreciate having read, *The Doctrines of Grace*.

–Myrue Spivey, Pastor
Grace Bible Sanctuary

The Doctrines of
GRACE

A Biblical Introduction

—*Chosen from the Foundation of the World*—

Roger W. F. Skepple

EDEN BOOK PRESS • MORROW GEORGIA

EDEN BOOK PRESS
Morrow, Georgia, USA

Unless otherwise noted, Scripture taken are from the *New American Standard Bible*, © 1960, 1962, 1963, 1968, 1871, 1972, 1973, 1975, 1977, by The Lockman Foundation. Used by permission.

ISBN 978-0998813806
Suggested Subject Headings: Theology, Doctrinal Studies, Calvinism, Election, Salvation, Soteriology, Doctrines of Grace, Reformed Theology, Reformation

© 1995, 2017
Revised Edition; Roger W. F. Skepple. All rights reserved. Printed in the United States of America.

Cover Designer: Joseph E. Banks

No part of this book may be reproduced without written permission, except for brief quotations in books and critical reviews.

Acknowledgments

Although the basics of the manuscript for *The Doctrines of Grace* was already completed, the expansion required a re-edit. That re-edit in some ways was more tedious that the original composition of the book. I would like to extend my thanks and gratitude to Cheryl Francis and Jana Riediger for their assistance in this regard. I would also like to thank Joseph Banks for lending his design skills for the new cover and his willingness to change his work as the book grew in size.

I would like to extend a special thanks to Steven Martin for writing the forward to this revised edition of my work. Steve has proved himself to be a faithful and encouraging brother to me throughout the years. He has and continues to fulfill the admonition of Hebrews 10:24 in my life, "and let us consider how to stimulate one another to love and good deeds." Thanks for your example and faithfulness in fulfilling your calling and ministry.

Finally, I would like to thank my wonderful wife who has been my faithful companion and steady friend throughout these thirty years of marriage and family. I truly would not be the man I am today or be fulfilling my calling without her support and encouragement. No truer words have been spoken regarding her than these, "An excellent wife, who can find? For her worth is far above jewels" (Prov. 31:10). Thanks Teresa.

Contents

Forward		11
Preface		15
Introduction to the Revised Edition		21
1.	The Doctrines of Grace	23
2.	The Sovereignty of God	27
3.	A Brief History of the Theological Discussion of The Doctrines of Grace	37
4.	The Doctrine of Total Depravity	43
5.	The Doctrine of Unconditional Election	51
6.	The Doctrine of Limited Atonement	69
7.	The Doctrine of Irresistible Grace	95

8.	The Doctrine of the Perseverance of the Saints	113
9.	Conclusion	135
10.	Appendix 1: The Christian's Confidence–A Brief Discussion of Christian Assurance	137
11.	Appendix 2: Causes of Salvation	161
12.	Appendix 3: Medium of Salvation	163
Notes		167

Foreword

You are holding in your hand a small book that can change your life. If you are already a Christian, it will show you the truly cosmic nature of the "good news" of Jesus Christ coming to earth, living a perfect life before God, dying on a Roman cross, rising from the dead and ascending back to heaven. If you are not yet a Christian believer, this book will show you why and how that must happen.

The most important question that every person must answer is: 'How can I be saved from the wrath to come?' If God is 'holy, holy, holy' and mankind is sinful, polluted, condemned and awaiting execution at the tribunal of God's justice, how can anyone stand before God?

Author Roger Skepple knows his Bible well, knows Christian history well and knows people all too well. He patiently shows us what is at stake and what God's Word teaches about how God originally created mankind, how our first parents fell into sin and took the whole world into enslavement to sin, how God had foreseen the Fall and already entered into a thoroughly worked out plan (covenant) to save a great multitude of sinners that no man can count from every tribe, tongue and people group on the planet.

What Pastor Skepple explains so well is that mankind has devised its own alternative gospel which is in fact no gospel at all. If mankind is spiritually dead in sin, blind to the truth of God, deaf to God's pleas and personally in rebellion against God, how in the world is that person going to save himself? Most people's New Year's resolutions don't last until February, how then are we to change ourselves? The Bible's answer is that God saves sinners. Not God saves sinners with their help, or people save themselves with God's help, but GOD SAVES SINNERS. That singular message is as new and powerful in our day as it was 500 years ago when Martin Luther began the Protestant Reformation. He and other Bible students of that day "protested" the false teaching of the medieval church and wanted to "reform" the practices of the medieval church that went along with the false teaching. The medieval church taught that Christ saves sinners with their help—a life of working to merit and earn favor with God. That would be a fool's errand to try to earn the grace of God. Luther and the other Protestant Reformers showed from the Bible that God saves sinners–period–without their help or earning anything. That's why its called 'sovereign grace' and not wages due.

When the truths in this book sink in, and I pray they will, you will pinch yourself when you lay in bed at night and ponder your life. Why was God merciful to me? Why in the world did God the Son, Jesus, come to live and die for a miserable, helpless sinner like me? Why did God not simply pass me by and leave me in my sins and condemnation? Would God Almighty go through all of this trouble and sacrifice for me? It truly is amazing grace!

Steve Martin
National Coordinator, Association of Reformed Baptist Churches of America (ARBCA)
Dean of Students, IRBS Theological Seminary

Preface

I had not initially intended to write a preface, however, when by brother in the ministry, Myrue Spivey, sent me his recommendation for the work, that all changed. After reading it, I thought that it actually encapsulated what I would have focused upon in a preface. So, I give you the full recommendation of my friend, Pastor Spivey:

When Pastor Skepple asked if I would be willing to read a manuscript of the revised version of his book, "The Doctrines of Grace" and pen a recommendation, I was both humbled and honored.

As I read through the manuscript, I was reminded of the intrigue, excitement, struggles, and at times, confusion I experienced as a young believer trying to get my mind around the doctrines of grace. I also remember the assurance, joy, contentment, and courageous conviction that flooded my soul when The Lord granted me grace to understand, accept and embrace these great truths. They are still as invigorating today as they were back then.

Currently, I am honored to serve as the teaching pastor of Grace Bible Sanctuary (GBS), a church that holds vigorously to the doctrines of grace. GBS is the same church in which The Lord, in His providence, was pleased to use my first wife, Patricia (deceased), and me to found nearly forty years ago. There are still points of theology, biblical verses and passages of Scripture that continue to intrigue me and get my spiritual juices going, and for this I give thanks and praise to the Lord Jesus.

One such passage is Jude 3, where Jude said, "Beloved, while I was very diligent to write to you concerning our common salvation, I found it necessary to write to you exhorting you to contend earnestly for the faith which was once for all delivered to the saints." I can't number the times I have read that verse. Yet, every time I read it, I am intrigued by the thought of the scores of controversial debates and the number of intense fellowships, (Christian angry disagreements), that could or would have been avoided in the body of Christ if Jude would have written what he says he was very diligent to write. I am even more intrigued that God who is sovereign, is the person who providentially put the divine pressure on Jude, causing him to change his subject and not write a definitive inspired book on salvation. Thus it is God's plan for each believer to personally study the Scriptures diligently, so that the Apostle Peter's words in 1 Peter 3:15 would be true of us. God also gave gifted men to His Church to equip (Ephesians 4:11-16), further establish, encourage, and strengthen believers in their faith (1 Thessalonians 3:1-3).

Pastor Skepple is one of those gifted men whom the Lord has given to the Church for this purpose. In writing his book, "The Doctrines of Grace," Pastor Skepple has made a great and lasting contribution to the Church of

Jesus Christ. Having been given the privilege to read Pastor Skepple's manuscript prior to it being published, in my estimation this book is bound to be used of God to establish, equip, encourage, and strengthen many of God's people, especially in their understanding of the doctrines of grace, and in their ability to articulate these blessed truths biblically, graciously, and lovingly to others in their spheres of influence.

I have not always embraced the doctrines of grace. Neither did any of the godly men who influenced me early after my conversion embrace the doctrines of grace. During my Bible school days I had only one professor that embraced these great truths. However, through providence, diligent study of the Scriptures, and through reading other godly men (who were pro and con toward the doctrines of grace), by God's grace I came to understand the doctrines of grace and embraced them.

As I read and reread Pastor Skepple's manuscript, I kept reflecting back on my own journey and thinking how helpful it would have been for me thirty years ago if I would have had a book on these great doctrines like Pastor Skepple's book. I do not say that to take away from any of the great theologians I consulted during my journey to the doctrines of grace. During my journey I had very little theology under my belt. Most of my biblical convictions at the time were at best vague, or the convictions of other men were my preferences. So my journey to embracing the doctrines of grace was one of long, arduous hours of labor as I grappled with these great truths.

Pastor Skepple has not shrinked back from presenting the whole counsel of God on this subject to his readers.

I thank and praise God for gifting Pastor Skepple with the ability to communicate high and lofty theological truths in such a clear, concise, correct, and readable way. I have read other books on the doctrines of grace during my journey, and although those books were excellent both biblically and theologically, the material was not presented as if it originated from a nurturing, pastor's heart. The Apostle Paul demonstrates this type of heart in 1 Thessalonians 2:7 where he says, "But we were gentle among you, just as a nursing mother cherishes her own children." A true pastor's heart is one which ministers to God's people with love, care, and great concern for His people. "The Doctrines of Grace" by Pastor Skepple is clearly written by one with a pastor's heart.

In his book, "The Doctrines of Grace," Pastor Skepple's theological scholarship shines through and he has held tenaciously to related biblical truths. Yet he has done so in such a compassionate way, that his love, care, and concern for the readers of his book emanates from its pages in such a way that even Christians who disagree with his conclusions will appreciate having read, "The Doctrines of Grace."

This is why I believe that through his book, "The Doctrines of Grace," Pastor Roger Skepple has made a noble contribution to the Church of Jesus Christ, and I believe that God will use his labors of love to help: establish, encourage, and strengthen many of God's saints -- young, old, pastors, missionaries, and theologians alike. Therefore, I am honored and grateful to our Lord for having been granted the privilege to recommend Pastor Roger Skepple's book, "The Doctrines of Grace." My prayer to God is that He will be pleased to use this book to edify, establish, encourage, and strengthen individuals, Sunday schools, and small group studies in an effort to help Churches embrace the doctrines of grace and solidify corporate unity on the doctrine of salvation and other glorious biblical truths in the local body, for His glory.

Introduction to the Revised Edition

There are multiple reasons why someone might want to republish a book, after it has accomplished what the author initially intended. When I originally published *The Doctrines of Grace*, my intent was to provide a small group of people I influenced with a resource that would lay out the biblical argument for these important Christian doctrines and the system they comprise.

The book was well received by friends and the small number of churches with which I had a relationship in the early 90's. The two small printings were easily exhausted. It was that response in the mid 90's that moved me to bring this work to the market again. Over the years the initial set of books had been read by the purchasers and shared with others leading to many requests for an expansion and a wider release. Self-publishing has changed in the two decades since I first brought this book out allowing for just such a wider release.

In the last two decades there have also been great changes in the world of reformed theology. It has seen unprecedented expansion, not just within the older paths in which it finds its "home," but even in new circles, reformational thinking has found a foothold and is expanding among the "young, restless, and reformed." I have watched these ideas become more accepted in the African-American community, of which I am a part; and watched the rise of the young reformers, who were sometimes more passionate than knowledgeable.

One thing that has been consistent throughout these twenty-some years since the first edition of *The Doctrines of Grace* is the continued need for works that focus on the biblical foundations of these critical doctrines. While doctrinal and theological works abound on the subject, simple biblical explanations of these grace doctrines that go beyond proof texts are still quite rare. This is where I believe this work still fits today. Each doctrine is examined from the vantage point of its biblical roots; and where necessary, opposition is addressed with the same eye to careful biblical explanation. It is my desire that *The Doctrines of Grace* will help you or someone you know have a greater biblical grasp on and appreciation of these grace-magnifying doctrines.

The Doctrines of Grace

Who is in control? No more basic a question is there that man seeks to know the answer to than this one. Christians have tended to answer this question with the unified answer of "God is in control." However, in making this statement, Christians do not always mean the same thing.

Some Christians view God's control as relative and reactive to man's exercise of freewill. In this position, God, in order to guarantee beings that have free choice, partially limits His control of the events of their life and decisions. Other Christians view God's control as absolutely independent of man's exercise of freewill. For this position, God executes His will in human history, to which man must conform. While conforming, however, they do not lose the trait of being responsible for their actions.

These two positions are expressed by the terms Arminianism, the first view explained, and Calvinism, the second view explained. Both positions received their designations from the proponents of these positions during the reformation of the church, in the sixteenth to seventeenth centuries. The two exponents were James Arminius and John Calvin. It is from Calvinism, the teachings of John Calvin, that the doctrines of grace are given explanation and support.

However, these views are late in the history of the church. The great divide between Arminianism and Calvinism existed early in the life of the church. Pelagius, who lived in the fourth and fifth centuries, and those who exposed his views in somewhat of a watered down fashion, conflicted over these very same issues with the great Christian theologian and pastor Augustine. It was from Augustine that John Calvin would depend heavily upon centuries later and to which John Arminius' semi-pelagian views took so much exception.

But the truth of these doctrines of grace are not ultimately dependent upon John Calvin and Augustine, for these men, and all those who adhere to teachings that could be labeled as similar to theirs, drew their teachings from the Holy Scriptures.

As noted above, Calvinism sees God as the Sovereign ruler of the universe executing His will in human history. As well as being applied to all the areas of Christian doctrine and belief, Calvinists also apply this truth to salvation. God is in sovereign control of the giving and receiving of salvation. Men do not come of their own accord, as the Arminian would say, and God reacts to them, but rather, God comes and man reacts to Him.

The application of the truth of God's sovereign control to the doctrine of salvation is explained by Calvinists with what they call the doctrines of grace. These doctrines have also been referred to as the Five Points of Calvin or Calvinism. These doctrines or five points are **T**otal Depravity, **U**nconditional Election, **L**imited Atonement, **I**rresistible Grace, and **P**erseverance of the Saints.

It will be noted that each of the first letters of each of these doctrines has been highlighted. That is because these doctrines have also been referred to by the acronym, **TULIP**. It should be noted at this point that Calvinism is not completely encompassed by just five doctrines.

Calvinism speaks to all the Christian doctrines and in fact may be said to be the most comprehensive expression of the Christian faith outside of the Bible. The focus of this book, however, is to introduce the reader to the doctrines of grace as taught in Scripture.

An attempt will be made to be thoroughly biblical in the proofs and explanations given in this book, because one of the foundational stresses of Calvinism is *Sola Scriptura*, which is Latin for "Scripture alone."

The Sovereignty of God

Before we can investigate the Doctrines of Grace, it would be helpful to first discuss the biblical doctrine of the sovereignty of God. The *Random House College Dictionary* gives one of the definitions of sovereign as, "having independent and self-governing power, status, or authority." In this definition, the power or authority that is possessed is independent, meaning that there are no forces outside the possessor of this power that determines its exercise.

It is also defined as being self-governing, meaning that how, when, and why it is exercised is totally self generated or decided. In this sense of sovereign, few

Christians would disagree that God is sovereign. However, the Bible goes much further than does the dictionary in defining and describing the sovereignty of God.

God's Control

That God is sovereign is often connected biblically with the concept of God having a plan, a comprehensive plan which incorporates all things. In the book of Isaiah, God stated that this was the case. Isaiah 46 dealt with the comparison between God and the idols of Babylon. Isaiah 46:1-2 focused upon the idols of Babylon, as to their inability to help the Babylonians in that they were in need of being carried, themselves. How could these idols, who needed to be carried, prevent the Babylonians from being carried away into captivity? God began addressing the people of God in 46:3.

God spoke first of Israel's special unchanging relationship to Him because He was the one who brought them into existence (46:3-4). As such, God would be the One who would deliver them from captivity (46:4). God then compared Himself with the idols of Babylon, making the statement in 46:5, "To whom would you liken Me, And make Me equal and compare Me." He was incomparable, because idols had human makers that had to take care of them (46:6-7). Therefore they offer no help in a time of distress (46:7).

God then began discussing Himself, calling His people to bring back to memory the type of God He was (46:8-9). He described Himself in verse 10 as the One who declared "the end from the beginning and from ancient times things which have not been done, saying 'My purpose will be established, And I will accomplish all My good pleasure.'" After describing the one whom He would send to deliver His people, He indicated "I have planned *it*, *surely* I will do it." Several things about God's plan become apparent from this passage.

First, God's plan is a comprehensive plan. Notice, according to Isaiah, that this plan encompassed the "end from the beginning." No part of that which fell between the end and the beginning falls outside of this plan.

Second, it was also called God's purpose. In other words, God had a specific purpose for the existence of the plan. He was attempting to accomplish something. Therefore He said that His purpose "will be established."

Third this plan was self determined. God said that He "will accomplish all My good pleasure." It is solely based upon God's will and no others. In other words, the sovereignty of God. Thus, it is clear that God has a plan by which He has established, for His own purposes, the individual events that will flow from the beginning to the end.

God Controls All Events

Although some would read the declaration made by God in Isaiah 46 and affirm that God was in control, they still might declare that this control only dealt with major issues having to do with the flowing of His plan of salvation. God's sovereignty, however, biblically speaking, affirms the reality that God is in control of all the events of human history. This control extends even to what might be labeled as minor events, as well as major events. The fact that God exerts His control over even minor events is seen in the biblical teaching which indicates that God is in control of even fortuitous events.

Demonstrated by Fortuitous Events

A fortuitous event, according to Charles Hodge, great theologian and former professor of Princeton Seminary, would be an event which depends "on causes so subtle and so rapid in their operation as to elude" human observation.[1] For example, the falling of a lot or a sparrow may be properly categorized as fortuitous. Is it possible to guess how a lot will fall or when and where a sparrow will fall to the ground? Impossible!

The Bible is expressly clear about these matters. As to the lot Proverbs 16:33 says, "The lot is cast into the lap, but its every decision is from the Lord." God is in control of even the lot. In reference to falling sparrows, the Bible says "Are not two sparrows sold for a cent? And yet not one of them will fall to the ground apart from your Father" (Mt. 10:29). Which sparrow falls, when it falls, where it falls, and how it falls are all under the control and guidance of our Father.

Beyond these two illustrations, one should also make note of the fact that such events as the random shooting of an arrow is controlled by God and the number of hairs on our heads at any particular moment is known by God (1 Kgs. 22:34; Mt. 10:30). It is absolutely clear from the Scriptures that God is a God of even the details, and nothing escapes His attention or control.

If God is concerned about the minor events of His universe, would He not be concerned about the major events also? Well, what is true of even the most fortuitous of events is true of every specific event that has, is, and will ever take place. We cannot possibly know all the reasons why God would bring about or permit every event that takes place, but we can know that He is in complete control. Particular events are clearly within the control of God. It is this belief that stands squarely in the minds and teaching of the Biblical authors. This fact is often manifested through Biblical prophecy.

Demonstrated by Biblical Prophecy

God's control of all the events of human history is the foundation of Him being able to expressly state what would and would not occur in the future. For example, in Genesis 15 when God sealed His covenantal agreement with Abram by the ratifying of a blood covenant, God declared to him, "And God said to Abram, 'Know for certain that your descendants will be strangers in a land that is not theirs, where they will be enslaved and oppressed four hundred years. But I will also judge the nation whom they will serve; and afterward they will come out with many possessions'" (15:13-14). Is God just guessing here?

If God had no control over world events, right down to the particular of minor events, how could He have possibly indicated so emphatically and assuredly that these particular events were going to take place? After all, Abram lived approximately 300 years prior to the bondage of Israel in Egypt. How many choices and decisions made in time could have influenced the choices that lead to Egypt's elevation in power and Abraham's decedents movement towards Egypt?

God Controls the Timing of All Events

Clearly then, human events are under the control of God. So particular is God that He has pinpointed events as to the particular moment that they are going to take place. This is quite clearly seen in the book of Revelation. In the ninth chapter of the book of Revelation, John gave his description of the sounding of the fifth and sixth trumpets and the events that ensue from that sounding. The sixth trumpet would deal with the killing of a third of mankind by four special angels who would facilitate the release of a massive army of 2,000,000. John's record of the release of these four special angels is instructive regarding this reality of God's comprehensive control.

In 9:14 the command to release these four special angels was foretold and then in 9:15 a description of these angels was given. It says, "And the four angels, who had been prepared for the hour and day and month and year, were released." The word "hour" was the Greek term used to describe the shortest period of time the Greeks reckoned. In modern language we may very well have translated this concept "the minute or second." This event is clearly to take place at a specific time, a time marked off as to the exact moment in human history.

Now, someone might raise an objection at this point and attempt to argue that God makes statements about these future events because He foresees them happening. Much like a sailor may use a telescope to foresee what is coming up next, so too God's foresight enables Him to tell what is going to happen next in human history.

While this hypothesis might sound good, this scenario, however, is completely unbiblical. Not only is such language and imagery never used in the Scriptures, but even beyond this, just the opposite is specifically taught and affirmed. Two examples should clearly bring out this reality.

First, in Daniel 2, after receiving the interpretation of King Nebuchadnezzar's vision, Daniel prayed and thanked God saying, "Let the name of God be blessed forever and ever, For wisdom and power belong to Him. And it is He who changes the times and the epochs; He removes kings and establishes kings; He gives wisdom to wise men, And knowledge to men of understanding" (2:20-21). The changing of the times and epochs and the changing of national entities, represented by their kings, is attributed not to the flow of history, but rather to God's active hand.

What Daniel prayed in the Old Testament, Jesus clearly and specifically affirmed in the New Testament. At the time of Jesus' ascension, after He had interacted with the disciples for some forty days (Ac. 1:3-5), He gathered them together for one last word before He would depart (1:9-11). At this final gathering the disciples had a question for Jesus recorded in 1:6, "And so when they had come together, they were asking Him, saying, 'Lord, is it at this time You are restoring the kingdom to Israel?'"

Jesus' intent for them was not to fixate on things that were out of their control, but rather to focus upon the mission of making disciples. This, He would indicate shortly, would be accomplished through them by the empowerment of the Holy Spirit (1:8; cf. Mt. 28:16-20). Jesus communicated before this, however, that the timing and implementation of events was God's, "He said to them, 'It is not for you to know times or epochs which the Father has fixed by His own authority'" (1:7).

In this verse, Jesus indicated that the times or epochs were "fixed by His own authority." Several important realities come forth from this statement. First, the events of human history are not a matter of man simply working out his own destiny by his control, but rather they are fixed. This term had two basic meanings, placing or laying something in the physical or spacial sense, or to make someone or something of someone. In this second meaning of the term, the concept of appointment or destiny comes into mind. This would have the meaning of making someone something by way of appointment. This is the idea that was being communicated here. The events of human history were established by appointment.

Second, the means that fixes, appoints, or establishes these events was God's authority. This statement aligns with the opening understanding of sovereignty that was identified earlier. Third, this authority is said to be God's "own authority" which also brings out the opening statement regarding the independent and self-governing power and authority that defines sovereignty.

Summary

By way of summary then, in reformed teaching, the sovereignty of God speaks to God's self-determined absolute control of the universe and its events, manifested through the eternal (Ps. 33:11; Ac. 15:18; Eph. 1:11; 2 Tim. 1:9) plan of God (Rom. 8:28; Eph. 1:11; 3:11) whereby based on His inscrutable wisdom, holiness, and goodness, He freely and without any basis outside of Himself sets for certain, without possible variation, what will come to pass in the universe (Isa. 14:26-27; 46:10-11; Dan. 4:35; Eph. 1:11).

One part of this eternal plan is God's plan of salvation. This plan is understood by reformed Christians through the medium of the doctrines of grace, or the five points of Calvinism. It is to these that we will now turn, looking first at the historical identification of the terminology and then the biblical basis of the doctrines.

A Brief History of the Theological Discussion of The Doctrines of Grace

The doctrines of grace did not become a prime expositional point within the reformation tradition in a vacuum, but rather they were brought to the forefront through a controversy within the Reformed branch of the reformation tradition. The two catalysts of the issue were Jacobus Arminius and Francis Gomarus, with the former being the primary focus at this point.

Jacobus Arminius, or James Arminius as he is often designated, was clearly a third generation Calvinist, follower of the Christian teachings of John Calvin. He was born in 1560 and obtained a completely thorough and pristine Calvinistic theological education at such institutions as the University of Marbury and Leiden, the academy of Geneva (under the tutelage of Calvin's successor, Theodore Beza), Basle, and Padua.[2]

Upon his return to Holland, his homeland, an important center of Reformed or Calvinistic thought,[3] he became a very influential and widely respected pastor of an important Reformed Amsterdam church. He also eventually became a professor at the University of Leiden in 1603, which he fulfilled until his death in 1609. It was because of his theological training and influence, that the church of Amsterdam asked of him a special duty, that would have implications that have lasted to this present day.

A certain Dirck Koornhart was advocating doctrinal positions about which the church had some serious questions. He was calling into question a number of the theological beliefs of Calvinism, especially that of predestination.[4] What started out as a thorough examination of Koornhart's views for the purpose of refutation, eventually turned into a shift in position, "after a struggle of conscience."[5] Arminius' shift of position and his public teaching of it at the university, set him at odds with Francis Gomarus, the other theology teacher at the university.

The debate between Gomorus and Arminius focused primarily upon the issue of predestination for in almost all of Arminius' other teaching he was essentially a strict Calvinist. But on the issue of predestination he rejected all facets of the Reformed understanding of it, although he did attempt to maintain a clear dependency of salvation upon the grace of God.⁶ The essence of the disagreement between the two professors was centered upon the basis of predestination not the fact of it.

Gomarus argued that before the decision to create was decreed, that is logically decided, a previous decision was made that God would be glorified in both predestination and reprobation. In his position election took place before both creation or the fall.⁷

Arminius' position was that the election of God was that Christ would be the Redeemer of lost mankind and predestination of humans for salvation was based on their foreseen faith in God.⁸ In his position those who were elected were those who were created, fell, and would exercise faith in Christ.

Arminius passed away at the height of this debate, but a couple things led to the continuation of the debate. He had managed to convert a number of Dutch pastors to his position. Also, the theological professor who replaced him also possessed his views.

With the passing of Arminius, his followers, referring to themselves as Arminians, took up one of his primary causes, which was an attempt to obtain a revision of two of the Dutch church's chief religious documents, the *Belgic Confessions* and the *Heidelberg Catechism*.⁹ To accomplish this, they submitted to the *States-General*, the governmental agency that exercised authority over the Dutch church, in 1610 a document known as a Remonstrance. The document contained five articles or points in which they differed from Calvinism:

> (1) Election and reprobation are founded on foreseen faith or unbelief. (2) Christ's death is for all, but only believers enjoy his forgiveness. (3) Fallen man cannot do good or achieve saving faith without the regenerating power of God in Christ through the Holy Spirit. (4) Grace is the beginning, continuation, and end of all good, but is not irresistible. (5) Grace can preserve the faithful through every temptation, but Scripture does not clearly say man may not fall from grace and be lost.[10]

The group from this point forward was known as the Remonstrants and at first received some favorable response, even convincing the civil authorities to outlaw the preaching of the doctrines that were contrary, which resulted in the punishment of Calvinists when they would not comply to the governmental stipulations.[11]

However, the situation for the Remonstrants regressed and the country was in severe turmoil. This led to the calling of an ecclesiastical assembly to hear the issue and a number of related issues, both political and religious in nature, that were connected to the Remonstrants' movement.[12]

One of the major concerns of the assembly beyond the five points of Arminianism was the Erastianism of the Netherlands, that is the control of the church by the state. The assembly was called the Synod of Dort and it commenced deliberations in November of 1618 and would continue until May of 1619. The assembly was convened with a mixture of both religious and secular leaders, both from the Netherlands and from several foreign countries.

The outcome of the Synod was a condemnation of the views of the Remonstrants and the affirmation of the five points that stood in contradiction to the five points of the self acclaimed Arminians. The five canons of Dort may be summarized as follows:

> (1) Unconditional election and faith are a gift of God. (2) While the death of Christ is abundantly sufficient to expiate the sins of the whole world, its saving efficacy is limited to the elect. (3, 4) All are so corrupted by sin that they cannot effect their salvation; in sovereign grace God calls and regenerates them to newness of life. (5) Those thus saved he preserves until the end; hence there is assurance of salvation even while believers are troubled by many infirmities.[13]

With the decision of Dort, the same rigors that were directed towards the Calvinists by governmental support of Arminians, were now directed towards the Arminians themselves. Some of the leaders were imprisoned or sentenced to death for treason, certain clergy were expelled from the country or faced imprisonment, and certain congregations were fined.[14] In due season, however, those rigors subsided with Arminianism being accorded official tolerance in 1631. Arminianism did not remain within the confines of the Reformed Dutch church as a splinter group, but extended beyond the Netherlands to have a significant influence upon English theology.[15]

The five points of Dort are what are defined today as the five points of Calvinism or the Doctrines of Grace and are the focus of this book. We might have wished that these titles were different, such as definite atonement rather than limited atonement and effectual calling rather than irresistible grace, yet these are the terms that have been bequeathed to us by history. When it is understood that these ways of describing these critical doctrines were forged in the context of conflict, they can be better appreciated for what they are, which are accurate, although not uncontroversial, explanations of truths of Scripture.

The Doctrine of Total Depravity

The doctrines of grace begin with the nature of mankind. Before the road map of God's grace can be traced, the question of the moral character or constitution of those upon whom this grace is to be bestowed must be answered. The affirmation of the Scriptures is that man is totally depraved.

In making this statement, it is not meant that man is always as bad as he could possibly be. That is, while man might not act as sinfully as he can all the time, sin has nonetheless infected every aspect of his existence. After all, not every human being is a serial killer or terrorist.

By *total* in total depravity it is meant that man in all his faculties, capabilities, passions, desires, functions and tendencies has been affected by sin. Man stands totally depraved before God in that his total being has been damaged and irrevocably altered from God's original creation. In order to see this, the post-fall nature of man and the nature of his need will be discussed.

The Post-fall Nature of Man's State

The term depraved appears in 2 Timothy 3:8. The term basically meant to completely destroy someone or something. When used figuratively as it is in 2 Timothy the focus was upon moral corruption. In Timothy this idea of moral corruption was applied to the unbeliever's mind. In other words, their thinking process and their thoughts, are morally reprobate.

This is supported, for example, in Ephesians 4:17-19, which referred to the unbeliever as living in the "futility of their mind, being darkened in their own understanding . . . because of the ignorance that is in them, because of the hardness of their heart . . . having become callous." Here we see a complete corruption of the human mind.

However, it is not just the mind of unsaved man that has a problem with moral corruption. It is also affirmed within the Scriptures that man's emotions are subject to moral corruption as well. As Jesus was coming to the end of His discussion with a man named Nicodemus in John 3, He made this statement regarding the unsaved, "And this is the judgment, that the light is come into the world, and men loved the darkness rather than the light; for their deeds were evil" (Jn. 3:19).

The intriguing issue about total depravity is that Jesus did not make a statement of comparative degree, such as "men loved the darkness more than the light." His statement was that men loved, *agapao* in the Greek, the darkness instead of the light. What we see here is contrast not comparison. This affection, love, originally intended to direct the human heart to admiration and respect of God, the One worthy of being judged to be of greatest value, this affection instead directs the human heart in just the opposite direction, towards darkness. Why is this the case?

All you need do is look at the bent of human behavior as an illustration of the bent of human affections. Jesus said, "for their deeds were evil." The proof positive for Jesus of His statement regarding man's truest love being darkness was his conduct. Jesus went on to indicate that their evil affections resulted in them being light haters, "For everyone who does evil hates the light, and does not come to the light, lest his deeds should be exposed" (3:20). Man's problem is that his affections are as evil as his conduct is.

But, not only are man's thinking and man's emotions subject to moral corruption, it is also indicated within the Scriptures that man's will is subject to moral corruption. The Bible affirms that man, if left to himself, will always and forever make the sinful choice against and in opposition to the good. What else should be expected from a person whose mind and affections are dominated and controlled by evil?

Thus, in Genesis 6:5, just before God destroyed the world by the flood, the following statement was made, "Then the Lord saw that the wickedness of man was great on the earth, and that every intent of the thoughts of his heart was only evil continually." By the use of three terms, translated as adjectives and an adverb in English, Moses demonstrated the depth of man's problem, "every . . . only . . . continually." The phrase "every intent" referred to all the wishes, wants, and desires of man's heart. The phrase "only evil" defined those wants and desires as being exclusively evil. Notice not a mixture or bent, but a full expression of evil. The final term, "continually," could be literally rendered "all the day long," which spoke to the unrelenting nature of man's evil bent.

Now, one might expect that the constant evil nature of man's conduct was somehow tied to man's lack of revelation or knowledge of the will of God. After all, the Bible was not written at this time, so man was unaware of God's design. With a change in his environment a bent towards the good would manifest itself.

This, however, is completely opposed to the revelation of Scripture. Even of the children of Israel in the Old Testament God had to say, "For My people are foolish, They know Me not; They are stupid children, And they have no understanding. They are shrewd to do evil, But to do good they do not know" (Jer. 4:22). Just a few chapters later God will proclaim in Jeremiah 13:23, "Can the Ethiopian change his skin Or the leopard his spots? Then you also can do good Who are accustomed to doing evil." As far as God is concerned mankind doing good is an impossibility.

The confession of David in Psalm 51:5 demonstrates that man does not develop into this problem through prolonged exposure to sin. Rather, just the opposite is the case. Mankind originates from the womb with just this bent. David wrote, "Behold, I was brought forth in iniquity, And in sin my mother conceived me." Man is born into this state of perpetual sin, he is a sinner from birth.

These same ideas are repeated with just as much vigor in the New Testament. Paul noted in 1 Corinthians 2:14, "a natural man does not accept the things of the Spirit of God." Paul affirmed in Romans 3:10-11 in perfect agreement with the Old Testament through quoting it, "as it is written, 'There is none righteous, not even one; There is none who understands, There is none who seeks for God; All have turned aside, together they have become useless; There is none who does good, There is not even one.'" The negations throughout this passage emphasize just how all encompassing these ideas really are. Further, unsaved man is in a condition of being enslaved to sin and free from righteousness according to Romans 6:20. Romans affirmed man's inability when it said, "because the mind set on the flesh is hostile toward God; for it does not subject itself to the law of God, for it is not even able to do so" (Rom. 8:7).

It could be argued at this point that the facts reveal a hole in this argument as it is presented. Although clearly man has a problem, this problem ought not be overstated, because the facts indicate that man does do some good things. This line of thought, however, reveals a failure to consider the nature of God as presented in the Scriptures.

Man can do externally good things, but because of his unsaved state, those deeds are not considered good by God because man does them for the wrong motives. In other words, good deeds devoid of good motives, that is the glory of God, fail to rise to the level of good as affirmed Scripturally. This is why Isaiah can say that this depravity is so pervasive that even the things that man does which may be considered righteous are tainted with uncleanness before an absolutely holy God (Isa. 64:6). What is the end point of this, if the nature of man is as presented?

The Nature of Man's Need

Possibly the most poignant summary of what total depravity means for man is found in the opening statement to the second chapter of Ephesians 2. There Paul summarized the nature of fallen man as follows,

> And you were dead in your trespasses and sins, in which you formerly walked according to the course of this world, according to the prince of the power of the air, of the spirit that is now working in the sons of disobedience. Among them we too all formerly lived in the lusts of our flesh, indulging the desires of the flesh and of the mind, and were by nature children of wrath, even as the rest (Eph. 2:1-3).

Paul stated here that man is dead. The idea of death is the cessation of life and therefore the inability to respond in the realm in which the death took place.

For example, to die physically does not mean that one ceases to exist all together, but rather that life in the context of the physical is no longer possible. We know that those who die physically still continue to exist in an immaterial form. Their human soul continues to exist. What their physical death means is that they are no longer able to respond to any stimuli whatsoever that sprung from the physical world. We could say that physical death renders one powerless and unable to respond to the physical world.

The idea of powerlessness and inability is important for understanding the nature of death. Death is not the reduction of capability to act within the realm in which the death took place. Neither is it a diminution or decrease in the ability to receive information broadcasted within the realm in which the death took place. Death, is the cessation of life and the complete inability to operate in any manner within the context in which the death took place.

Clearly, this death was not physical since, according to Paul, man yet walked. Obviously this is not a physical death, but rather a spiritual one. This is supported, of course, by the death being defined as "in your trespasses and sins." This death, although spiritual, had influence in the physical world because it served to define the nature of man's conduct. This death imbues the conduct, "walked," of the unbelieving world in such a manner that it makes sin the only defining reality of their existence.

Thus, from the Scriptures it might be concluded that man is more than just sinfully weak or a little sick. Rather, man is dead, spiritually speaking, that is born completely or fully corrupted. Every facet of his existence, what makes him who he is has been tainted by sin. Now, all he can do is choose darkness over the light, for he is unable and unwilling to choose the light. For this reason it must be affirmed, not only is man depraved, but he is totally so. As such, because his will is linked inseparably to his nature all of his choices, decisions, motives, and actions are evil, just as his nature is evil.

Thus, if man's problem is spiritual death, then his need must be spiritual life. Remaining in the state in which he is, man would be unable to go to heaven, because when faced with choosing Christ (good), and choosing evil (rejecting Christ), he would always choose evil. That means that all men could be rightfully sent to hell by God, without there being any injustice in God at all. As Paul plainly stated, "For the wages of sin is death" (Rom. 6:24).

Therefore, if God desired that there be some people in heaven, a plan would have to be made that guaranteed such. If man is to be saved, which requires a good decision, (a decision to turn to Christ, to choose and follow through with doing good), then something must happen with his will. The only source of good is God, so if something good is going to take place, it must come from Him. Such takes place in God's act of unconditional election, the next doctrine in the doctrines of grace.

The Doctrine of Unconditional Election

Enter God's elective choice. For man to be saved his will must be changed from choosing evil to choosing good. Exactly whom will have their wills positively affected, so as to be able to choose to do the good, which in their unsaved state, they cannot choose? The doctrine of election demonstrates the fact that God sovereignly chooses, based on nothing in those chosen (but solely upon His will), those who are to be born again.

Although some do not think of this doctrine in positive terms, such reveals a complete misunderstanding of this doctrine and failure to think of it in purely biblical categories. Take, for example, the fact that for someone like the apostle Paul, election was often expressed within the context of thanksgiving. So, at the beginning of his great hymn of praise in Ephesians 1, Paul wrote,

> Blessed be the God and Father of our Lord Jesus Christ, who has blessed us with every spiritual blessing in the heavenly places in Christ, just as He chose us in Him before the foundation of the world, that we should be holy and blameless before Him. In love He predestined us to adoption as sons through Jesus Christ to Himself, according to the kind intention of His will, to the praise of the glory of His grace, which He freely bestowed on us in the Beloved (1:3-6).

Twice in this opening statement, Paul made note of the believer being chosen (1:4) and being predestined (1:5), both of which drew praise from Paul in 1:3 and ought to draw praise from the believer in 1:6.

But this was not the only place where Paul expressed this type of exuberance regarding this critical doctrine. He indicated to the Thessalonians in his opening thanksgiving section, that he gave thanks to God for them (1:2), "knowing, brethren beloved by God, His choice of you" (1:4). Thanksgiving was also a part of his reminder to them of their election in 2 Thessalonians 2:13, when he wrote, "But we should always give thanks to God for you, brethren beloved by the Lord, because God has chosen you from the beginning for salvation through sanctification by the Spirit and faith in the truth." Within this statement the Bible clearly pointed out the fact of the believer's election.

The Fact of the Believer's Election

Paul, with no debate and no defense, simply wrote, "God has chosen you." There is more than one Greek term used for the idea of God's choice of the believer, Paul used *haireo* here, the more unique of these terms. It was a word that referred to the idea of to take, win, or seize something. The form that Paul used in this particular text led to this term meaning "to take to oneself" or "to select" for oneself. In other words, the action was done for the benefit of the person performing the action.

When used in this manner, its context dealt with the selection between two options or possibilities. We see this use, for example, in non-salvation contexts when Paul wrote in Philippians 1:22 regarding his struggle to either go to be with the Lord or to remain and continue ministry here on earth, "But if I am to live on in the flesh, this will mean fruitful labor for me; and I do not know which to choose." This same idea of choosing between two possibilities is found in Hebrews 11:25, when the author said the following regarding Moses' selection to side with his people, rather than with the Egyptians, "choosing rather to endure ill-treatment with the people of God, than to enjoy the passing pleasures of sin."

It should be clear from these two other uses of this particular term in the New Testament that the idea was to select for oneself. This term has the same meaning in this context, which was focused upon spiritual identity. In other words, how did the Thessalonians become a part of God's family, how did they become a part of the "beloved," a term which Paul used in the first half of the statement to describe them? God selected them for Himself.

This is the only meaning for this idea that is possible in the Bible. It does not matter whether this word or the other main term used for the idea of "chosen" in the Bible, *eklegomai*, when used of God it always referred to selection by God for whatever was the focus. So, whether it was national election, as in the case of Israel (Ac. 13:17; Deut. 10:15), vocational election, as in the case of the apostles (Jn. 6:70; Ac. 9:15), situational election, as in the case of Peter being the one to take the gospel to the Gentiles (Ac. 15:7), or positional election, as in the case of the holy angels (1 Tim. 5:21), God is always the one doing the choosing.

All the types of choosing identified in the Bible, including choosing for salvation which is the focus in 2 Thessalonians 2:13, have as their perspective God's choosing or selecting for the particular purpose identified in the context.

Now, this is an important realization due to the sloppy religious language used by many believers who describe their salvation as "I chose God" or "I chose to follow Christ." The problem with this language is that the Bible never, ever uses the words for choose or any of its derivatives in reference to salvation with man as the subject.

If there was any choosing being done, biblically, it is always, without exception, attributed to God and never to man. In fact, of the more than twenty occurrences of these terms in contexts dealing with salvation in the New Testament every single occurrence, without exception, is attributed to God. So, although such individuals may be well meaning in the statement, they are actually misdirected in their understanding of this biblical concept.

God chooses, the believer receives (Jn. 1:12). This is an undeniable fact that the Scriptures teach. That election is a teaching of the Bible, must be believed and affirmed if one desires to be a biblically literate Christian. Now, believers may differ on what it means, but they cannot differ on whether it exists, for the Bible clearly teaches it.

To say that one does not believe in election is like saying that they do not believe in justification. Both are clearly mentioned and taught in the Bible. Although believers might have differences of opinion on the list of spiritual benefits that happen at the moment of justification and those that happen after it, they cannot deny that the Bible teaches it. If two believers disagreed on justification, then one of them would be wrong. The same is true of election. It is a fact of the Bible. There might be disagreement on how it is defined, but it cannot be denied. If two believers were to disagree on its meaning, one of them would be right and the other one would be wrong.

The Time of the Believer's Election

The natural question that comes to a person's mind when they realize the validity of this critical doctrine relates to its timing, when it occurred. Paul, himself, in his statement on election in 2 Thessalonians, answered that question as well, when he noted that they were chosen "from the beginning." This raises another question, however, which is the beginning of what?

This is clearly a general phrase which was used in many different ways throughout the New Testament and basically draws its meaning from the particular context in which it appears. So, some ways in which it was used were to refer to the beginning of creation (Heb. 1:10), the beginning of Jesus' ministry (Lk. 1:2), or the beginning of being a Christian (1 Jn. 2:24). The context is determinative for telling us what type of beginning is being discussed. So, Paul could either mean that the Thessalonians were selected by God from the beginning of their salvation or from the beginning of time.

The key here in helping us to comprehend which of these designations is being described is Paul's other uses of the idea of "chose" in salvific contexts. The most important of these for understanding this phrase is Ephesians 1:4, when he reminded the Ephesians that they should praise God for His blessing (1:3), first on the list being, "just as He chose us in Him before the foundation of the world, that we should be holy and blameless before Him. In love."

The phrase "the foundation of the world" is a reference to the creation. Throughout the creation story in Genesis 1-2, God was pictured as a Fashioner and Builder. He formed the man in Genesis 2:7 and fashioned or built the woman in 2:22. The Jews understood God to be a Master Builder, an Architect and therefore they pictured the creation as a building needing to be founded. Psalm 24:1-2 says, "The earth is the Lord's, and all it contains, The world, and those who dwell in it. For He has founded it upon the seas, And established it upon the rivers." Proverbs 3:19 says, "The Lord by wisdom founded the earth; By understanding He established the heavens." God says of Himself when speaking to Job, "Where were you when I laid the foundation of the earth" (38:4)?

So, Paul here was referring to the creation of the world before anything was made, before anyone existed, before sin, before the fall, before mankind. In other words, in eternity past, when all that existed was God, He selected for Himself those who would be saved. Interestingly, this was not the only thing that took place in this era. The provision of Christ to be the sacrifice for sin was also made by the Father during this time period according to 1 Peter 1:19-20. With the individuals having been chosen and the provision for them made, all before the creation, God then at that same time also wrote the individuals names who would be the objects of His choosing in the book of life.

This reality is expressed in Revelation 13:8, where John wrote, "And all who dwell on the earth will worship him, everyone whose name has not been written from the foundation of the world in the book of life of the Lamb who has been slain." The same idea was basically repeated with slight differences in 17:8. The people who were being discussed were those who would dwell on the earth, who were related to the beast of the Revelation in some fashion. These individuals were said not to have had their name written "in the book of life." In 13:8 this book of life was said to be, "of the Lamb who has been slain," obviously a reference to Christ. These texts were referring to, then, the wicked who, not being Christians, would therefore not have their names written in Christ's book.

Thus, with the individuals chosen, the provision made, the names written down, all before the creation, God further prepared their inheritance at that same time for Jesus said that when He would return and judge the saved and unsaved that "Then the King will say to those on His right, 'Come, you who are blessed of My Father, inherit the kingdom prepared for you from the foundation of the world'" (Mt. 25:34).

Sometime before time and everything else was created, God possessed in His mind, hidden away, a plan (cf. Mt. 13:35). In that plan, He determined to create and to allow the fall of angels and the eventual fall of mankind. Part of that plan would also include the salvation of human beings. And at that time, "before the foundation of the world," that is "from the beginning," He selected or picked out those who would be saved. The truth is plainly laid out for believers on the pages of Scripture.

The Purpose of the Believer's Election

If it is not obvious by now, the purpose of election was for the salvation of a human soul. Paul clearly identified this as he noted in 2 Thessalonians 2:13, "for salvation." Of course, this has already been the undercurrent in this passage, but with this statement there is no longer any doubt as to what the focus of the apostle Paul was in writing on these issues.

The meaning of this term and the family of terms of which it is a part, is saving or keeping someone from serious peril. As such it was used of rescuing someone from the peril of death. It quite easily transferred into the religious sense of saving one from the serious spiritual peril of hell. However, it was not one being saved from hell that was the emphasis of the New Testament usage of this word. The key to understanding the full nature of salvation or salvation from sin, which often describes it, is comprehending that the individual from which one was being saved ultimately, was God.

In Romans 5, Paul used one of the terms from this family in making the following statement regarding believers, "Much more then, having now been justified by His blood, we shall be saved from the wrath of God through Him" (5:9). What is this idea of God's wrath and its extension towards mankind? The idea of the wrath of God can refer to one of three things: 1) God's temporal wrath, which is His removal of His restraining grace (Rom. 1:18); 2) God's eschatological wrath, which is the great and terrible Day of the Lord (Zeph. 1:15; Rev. 16:1); and 3) God's ultimate wrath, which is hell (Rom. 9:22; Eph. 2:2-3).

That which ties each of these manifestations of the wrath of God together is the fact that they are the outgrowth of God's divine condemnation on and judgment on sin and the sinner. The wrath of God is a terrifying reality. The author of Hebrews summarized what the human recognition of this reality should be when he wrote, "It is a terrifying thing to fall into the hands of the living God" (10:31). This, however, does not encompass the full scope of the fact of man's real problem. God's wrath was being expressed towards him in time and would result in a cataclysmic climax of eternal condemnation, if he was not saved from it.

The Author of the Believer's Election

Throughout these passages, the Bible has affirmed over and over again that God was the one who elected believers for salvation. But, we as Christians serve a triune God, so it is no surprise that all three members of the Trinity can be identified as playing a role in the outworking of God's elective plan. So, the Father chose and predestined before creation, the provision of the means was placed on the shoulders of the Son before creation and the elected names were recorded in His book, while the Holy Spirit's work of separation, as 2 Thessalonians 2:13 indicated, was applied in time to separate the elect from the masses of lost humanity and to save them.

Interestingly enough, all three of the persons and their role in the outworking of the plan of election was recorded in one verse, 1 Peter 1:1-2, in which Peter stated, "Peter, an apostle of Jesus Christ, to those who reside as aliens, scattered throughout Pontus, Galatia, Cappadocia, Asia, and Bithynia, who are chosen according to the foreknowledge of God the Father, by the sanctifying work of the Spirit, that you may obey Jesus Christ and be sprinkled with His blood: May grace and peace be yours in fullest measure."

The working of the Godhead is harmonious and integrated. Theologians refer to this as the doctrine of the economical trinity, that is the working of God with the economy, which means the universe He created. When God works with His creation there is order, actions are carried out of God, through the Son, by the Spirit, unto the Father. In other words, God comes up with the plan, the Son provides the means for the plan being worked out, and the Spirit actively carries the plan out, and it is all done for the Father's glory. Whether it is the atonement or creation or anything else that God does. Election is no different.

In 1 Peter 1:2 Peter instructed his recipients on the role of each person of the Godhead in bringing them to salvation, the objective of them being chosen. Peter began 1:2 with God's plan. The words "according to" identify for the readers that Peter was going to give them what the bases for their election was. What was the basis or foundation of their election? It was "the foreknowledge of God the Father." This word, "foreknowledge," is best rendered foreordination and means much more than to know something before it happens.

The word that has been translated foreknowledge was used only seven times in the New Testament. Five times as a verb and only twice in its noun form. One of its noun uses occurred here in 1 Peter and the other in Acts 2:23. It will be noticed that the context of that verse was Peter delivering his Pentecost sermon. As he came to the events of Jesus Christ's life over the three previous years culminating in His death, burial and resurrection and declared, "this Man (Jesus), delivered up by the predetermined plan and foreknowledge of God, you nailed to a cross by the hands of godless men and put Him to death."

For a clear understanding of the first half of this verse one must look at the phrase, "the predetermined plan and foreknowledge of God." In the Greek language there existed a method whereby two nouns would be used to describe the same act by a simple construction. The two nouns which described this thing would be put in the same grammatical case, separated by an "and," and then finally, the first noun would be given an article. When this occurred, the reader knew that the author was using these two nouns to describe the same thing. This is the situation that we have in Acts 2:23.

Luke, the author of Acts, has used this construction to show that God's predetermined plan and foreknowledge are the same act. The word "plan" means the exchange of deliberative judgment, while "determined" means to put limits on something. Here, it was in a form which showed it had the present result that a certain thing had been appointed or decreed. So, foreknowledge, used here, referred to that counsel of God, in which after deliberative judgment, Jesus was delivered into human hands to be crucified. The noun clearly means foreordination.

In four of the six cases in which this word was used this was the meaning, every one of these times the one who foreknew was God. The other two times it simply meant knowledge before hand, and spoke of human beings being the knowers.

In 1 Peter 1:2, foreknowledge referred to that counsel of God in which after deliberative judgment certain from mankind were chosen to a certain position, which is defined in this context as salvation. What was the basis of this choosing? Just as in the case of Christ, it was all dependent upon God's choice and will, so it was here in this verse. So the basis of their election was God's foreordination. They were foreknown by God because they were foreordained by Him to salvation.

Something should be noted, here, before moving on to Peter's next phrase. The concept of foreknowledge was used again later in this very chapter when Peter wrote regarding Christ, "For He was foreknown before the foundation of the world, but has appeared in these last times for the sake of you" (1:20). To know before hand when used of God, has to mean to foreordain and not to foresee, as some would like it defined.

Next Peter dealt with the role of the Holy Spirit in the election of his recipients. He said that they were chosen by the "sanctifying work" of the Spirit, which was the same basic point Paul had made in 2 Thessalonians 2:13. Sanctify means to set apart or consecrate something. The sinners which God the Father foreordained to salvation are set apart for salvation by the Holy Spirit. This is not speaking of the actual act of salvation, which is spoken of next, but rather the sanctification previous to salvation of the sinner.

The sanctifying work of the Holy Spirit evidences four different types of sanctification: 1) preparational; 2) positional; 3) practical; and 4) prospective. This verse speaks of the first, preparational. This speaks to the act of God whereby the Holy Spirit sets the unbeliever apart from the potential realm of condemnation for the actual realm of salvation. So the work of the Spirit in Peter's recipients being chosen is that He is the One that marked or set them apart for something which is defined by the context as salvation.

After dealing with the Holy Spirit, Peter moved on to discuss Christ's role, "that you may obey Jesus Christ and be sprinkled with His blood." The obedience that Peter wants to specify here was not the obedience the believer has to Christ as His head, the obedience of the faith. Rather, the focus here was the obedience of the sinner which brings the actualization of salvation, the obedience to the faith. We are sprinkled with His blood at salvation. This imagery was drawn from the Old Testament practice of dedicating something to the Lord. Sprinkling it with blood transferred it from common use to God's use.

Peter's line of thought has focused upon working through the events that made his recipients chosen and eventually led to their salvation. This is evident because this obedience is answered by the sprinkling of Jesus' blood, which is in the next phrase.

So the purpose of them being foreordained by God and set apart by the Spirit, is in order that they may come to the place of putting faith in Jesus Christ. The act of faith brings the sprinkling of the blood of Jesus Christ. This pictures the act of Moses as well as the Levitical priesthood whereby they sprinkled the people in order to cleanse them and according to the Law to forgive sin. Hebrews 9:11-22. Christ, the mediator of the new covenant, cleanses and forgives the sinner, who comes to Him in faith.

Peter has taught his recipients what the role of each of the persons of the God-head is in their being chosen ones of God. God the Father foreordained them to salvation, the Holy Spirit separated them to obedience or faith in Christ, and Jesus Christ cleanses them with His blood. These facts, however, are not just true for those Peter wrote to, but for all those who are chosen. If you are chosen, which you are if you are saved, this verse applies to you as well.

The Outcome of the Believer's Election

Romans 8:29-30 clearly outlined both the beginning point and the ending point of God's plan of election. In this statement we see the intended outcome. This passage is part of a broader context which dealt with the believer's complete assurance that everything was going to be alright in his life. The believer could be assured that *It's going to be alright* because God has, in His infinite and unfathomable love (8:39), provided him with His Divine Paraclete (8:26-27),[16] has brought him to Himself through His Divine Plan (8:28-30), and has guaranteed his destiny by His Divine Protection (8:31-39). Paul begins this section in 8:26.

The first part of this verse seemed to refer back to groaning of both the created order, as well as mankind himself. This groaning was in reference to man's **already but not yet** disposition due to salvation. So the emphasis was man's weakness due to the fact that he was a sinner saved by grace, and as such he did not know the types of things he should request. (Not so much how to pray, but for what to pray). Just as creation testified to this fact by groaning, so the Holy Spirit.

These groanings have nothing to do with the speaking of tongues, they were not heard by man, they were heard by God (cf. 8:27). This God, Paul said, in 8:27, was the very One who was involved in the granting of the prayer based on that which was communicated, Himself being intimately knowledgeable or related to the Spirit who was doing the interpreting. In turn, the Spirit who was doing the interpreting was intimately familiar with the will of God who was doing the granting. So the believer could be assured that there was all the potential in the world for his prayers to be made and answered.

In 8:28 Paul then taught that God's plan took into account all the things that happen to the believer. Some view the "good" here as referring to the believer's ultimate good despite the individual events not necessarily being good. While this is definitely conceivable, it could also be conceived as being God's good. The meaning would thus be that God would take all the events of the believer's life and work them together for His good plan. In other words, God's working is bigger than the individual believer's life. His plan has ultimately all glory going to Himself and no other (cf. Ex. 20:5).

This latter option fits the mood of the context best, which focuses on God's divine plan and divine provision, which is also seen in the first eight chapters of this book. This should be the believer's ultimate focus anyway, the glory of God, not the glory of himself. This is only applicable to those who are in a love relationship with God due to the divine call to His divine purpose.

Paul then moved on in our key verse to explain this special relationship. These next two verses obviously explain or give the reason for 8:28, due to the fact that 8:29 begins with the explanatory conjunction "for." Why was it that God had irrevocably tied Himself to these people? He had done it because, He had planned for a specific end for their lives (the image of His Son), which in turn was not for their glory but for His Son's (that He might be *firstborn*–which speaks to a unique special position, preeminent).

This verse teaches that the ones who were foreknown by God, He predestined. Foreknowledge, as indicated above, was not just knowing something before it happened, but when speaking of God in reference to people it referred to that counsel of God by which after deliberative judgment certain individuals were linked to Himself. These individuals were thus predestined in order to guarantee that they become conformed to Christ's image. To predestine means to mark someone or something out with a boundary before doing something with or to that someone or something.

Romans 8:30 followed-up on the idea of God predestinating, and, with the ultimate statement of divine order and plan, gave a clear and sequential account of God's divine working in the believer's life. Beginning with eternity past (the plan; predestined), Paul moved to the historical past (the implementation of the plan; called), to the historical present (the outworking of the plan; justified), to the definite future (the consummation;

glorified). It should be noted in this sequence that the idea of called was not the general call that every man receives. Rather, it was the effectual call of God that only the elect receives. We know this because it always results in justification. This, the biblical calls, will be discussed in a more indepth fashion later.

This was the *divine turnpike*–there was no exit. The only way to get access to the plan was to be foreknown and predestined, the only way to exit was to be glorified with God. One cannot begin the process, it must be begun for him in eternity when God selected him out for salvation.

Summary

God has, based upon His own will, chosen those whom He will save. This choosing took place before the world was even created and is part of God's irrevocable plan. His goal in doing this is to bring those whom He has elected to conformity to the image of His Son. The next question to be answered, then, is upon what basis can such an act be made. Once chosen, upon what basis will God reconcile? This moves us to the doctrine of limited atonement.

The Doctrine of Limited Atonement

Just choosing someone for salvation would not be sufficient in itself, for man's total corruption and the impact of sin necessitated certain things. Such things as his sin as a violation of God's law be paid for, as his being an object of God's wrath be reversed, and as his standing before God as a sinner be changed. If man paid for his own sin, he would have to do so in hell forever, thus he could not in turn be saved.

So, since God had determined that He was going to save some, there had to be a way by which such a rescue could be orchestrated. That way would be through what the Old Testament refers to as an act of atonement, and what the New Testament clearly attributed to the death of Christ. In order to understand this terminology we must first understand what the atonement is, and then why it is limited.

The Atonement of Jesus Christ

There are many terms which the Bible uses to describe the work of Christ on behalf of the sinner. Such terms as redemption, justification, and propitiation appear throughout the writings of the New Testament authors and such concepts as ransom and substitution are linked to His death. All evangelicals believe that at its very foundation, Christ's death provided both expiation and propitiation for man's sin.

Paul summarized this fact when he wrote, "For what the Law could not do, weak as it was through the flesh, God did: sending His own Son in the likeness of sinful flesh and as an offering for sin, He condemned sin in the flesh" (Rom. 8:3). It can simply be said that Jesus' death was the divine answer for sin. To understand this, both the basis of the atonement and the nature of the atonement must be comprehended.

The Basis of the Atonement

The basis of the atonement of Christ must be found first and foremost in the Father. Because it is a divine act carried out on the behalf of men, being initiated by the incarnation of Christ (Heb. 2:9-18; 10:1-18), it must find its foundation within the character of God Himself. Although when God acts, He acts as a person, with all of Himself being engaged and active, there are two of His attributes that particularly stand out as the impetus for the atoning work of the Lord Jesus Christ. They are God's love and God's justice.

Although this verse is often abused and rarely fully understood as to its true significance, it cannot be doubted that this text, John 3:16, makes it absolutely clear that the atonement is the work of a loving God. Jesus told Nicodemus, in explanation of the fact that He was the source of eternal life to all who look to Him in believing faith that, "God so loved the world, that He gave His only begotten Son, that whoever believes in Him should not perish, but have eternal life."

As important and significant as love was to the foundation of the atonement, such a foundation is absolutely incomplete and inadequate without the second attribute that played just as important a role in the atonement. It is at this point that many modern evangelicals have ceased to live up to the full message of the New Testament regarding the atonement. For, just as love is a motivating principle for the atonement, justice is likewise a vital motivational element as well.

The reason that the Christian gospel does not deteriorate into so much religious sentimentality is because God's answer to man's sin was initiated both by God's love and His justice. This is the message of Romans 3:25-26 in which Paul says of Christ, "whom God displayed publicly as a propitiation in His blood through faith. This was to demonstrate His righteousness, because in the forbearance of God He passed over the sins previously committed; for the demonstration, I say, of His righteousness at the present time, that He might be just and the justifier of the one who has faith in Jesus."

The atonement was to demonstrate that God was not a reckless Judge. Only a reckless, irresponsible judge would pass over infractions of His own law without eventually exacting any punishment. For law to be law it must have a penalty for infractions against it. Christ came and laid down His life so that the Father would be a credible judge and it might be plainly clear that the Father was both "just and the justifier."

He both punished and requited, carried out both of these realities, within the parameters of the law system that He established to regulate the world. He punished Christ as a substitute for the sin of the guilty, and then took the perfect life and righteousness of Christ and forensically (legally) applied it to those whose guilt had been placed upon Christ. Here then is the basis of the atonement, plainly demonstrated.

But why was something as radical as Christ's death necessary? Does the Bible indicate that Christ's death was necessary? The answer to these questions can be confusing. Christ's death was not necessary, but it was also necessary. Can both of these statements be true? Absolutely.

First, Christ's death was not necessary. The fact of the matter is, since salvation is by grace, that is unmerited favor, God could have chosen to not extend it to man and could have rightly left man in his fallen condition and done nothing to change it. This would have resulted with every human person ending up in hell. This would have been the just thing to do. God would have been perfectly just and perfectly fulfilled in doing this, since He is self-existent and perfectly, righteously, and rightly satisfied with Himself. In this sense then, the atonement did not have an independent necessity to it.

However, it is also true that the atonement was necessary. By this it is meant contingently necessary. Contingent or dependent upon what? Once the divine decision was made in eternity past to save some of Adam's helpless race, that decision in turn determined the means by which that salvation would have to take place. The salvation of men would require the death of a man; and the reconciliation of men with God would require a divine mediator.

The atonement accomplished by Jesus Christ became necessary because God chose to save some. According to the author of Hebrews, Christ's sacrifice was necessary for Hebrews 2:17 says, "Therefore, He had to be made like His brethren in all things, that He might become a merciful and faithful high priest in things pertaining to God, to make propitiation for the sins of the people." Why is it that He "had to be made like His brethren"? The author of Hebrews indicated one of the reasons why in 10:4, the blood of bulls and goats was insufficient for the task of salvation.

Once the plan was set in eternity past, the death of the Messiah, Jesus Christ, was demanded due to the inevitability of the working out of God's plan. Is it possible for the thwarting of God's plan? Absolutely not! Thus Jesus told the two disciples on the road to Emmaus,

"And He said to them, 'O foolish men and slow of heart to believe in all that the prophets have spoken! Was it not necessary for the Christ to suffer these things and to enter into His glory'" (Lk. 24:25-26)? Did not Jesus Himself recognize that it was the will of God that was the determining factor in His ensuing death when He prayed, "My Father, if it is possible, let this cup pass from Me; yet not as I will, but as Thou wilt" (Mt. 26:39). The fact that Christ died is evidence enough that the will of God was for such to take place.

It is a true statement to say, therefore, that Christ's death and the atoning work that it accomplished was both ultimately unnecessary and contingently necessary at the same time. So the basis of and necessity of the atonement is clearly seen. What of its significance and nature? There is a key phrase that leads the believer into a clear understanding of the nature of the atonement. Paul used this phrase in Ephesians 5:2 when he stated that "Christ also loved you, and gave Himself up for us." The key phrase is "for us," which contains a wealth of meaning and import.

The Nature of the Atonement

First, this phrase, "for us," represented the fact that the atonement was both penal and triumphant. We say this because it was "for us" in the sense that it was "for our sins." As we read earlier in Hebrews, it was "for the sins of the people." Man both possessed a sin nature which meant that he was completely corrupted and bound by sin and he also was held guilty by God of Adam's first sin (Rom. 5:12-21). Both of these realities were dealt with in

Christ's sacrifice. Christ's sacrifice was penal in nature, that is it satisfied the demands of God's justice as a judge. As we saw in Romans 3, a judge cannot just simply dismiss the charges against a convicted criminal. The crime must be paid for. Yet it was us convicted criminals who were in need of the charges being dismissed against us. The sacrifice of Christ allowed God to both have His justice as a judge satisfied, yet also supply salvation for the convicted criminal.

It made freedom from sin's domination possible for those who place their faith in Christ. The dominion of sin was complete and thorough in the life of the unsaved person, dominating him both internally and externally as passages like Ephesians 4:17-19 indicate. So, what could possibly break sin's stronghold and mastery?

Freedom from sin is only possible through death. Paul says in Romans 6:7, "he who has died is freed from sin." God's response in Christ's sacrifice is to identify the sinner with Christ so that he might experience the death that Christ experienced. The old man was crucified with Christ and the old man's death meant that sin's domination and mastery was broken (Rom. 6:1-6). So Christ's triumph becomes the believer's triumph. So the atonement was both penal and triumphant.

Christ's atoning work is such that it needed not to be repeated, it is sufficient within itself to accomplish all that God meant for it to accomplish. This is in stark contrast to the sacrifices of the Old Testament sacrificial system. Those sacrifices were offered repeatedly on a daily, weekly, monthly, and yearly basis. The mere fact that they had to be repeated and that they were the very same sacrifices speaks to their inadequacy to accomplish any type of long term solution for sin. The author of Hebrews asks that if they had been adequate then "would they not have ceased to be offered, because the worshipers, having once been cleansed, would no longer have had consciousness of sins" (10:2)? Christ's sacrifice on the other hand was final (10:5-14). Truly indeed, He loved us.

Even further than this, Christ's atonement was also substitutionary and vicarious. Let us take some time here to explain these two important aspects of Christ's death. Being that God is the Sovereign Ruler and Lord of all mankind and that His will, which is a reflection of His own perfect nature, is the sole standard of right and wrong, then all men are born under an obligation to live according to His will (Ps. 24:1-2; 47:7-9; Eph. 1:11; Lev. 19:2). Any failure to adhere to His will must be punished in order to maintain the standard of His will and the holiness of His nature. An unpunished violation of His will would mean that His will was free to be ignored and that there was some other standard outside of His nature to which mankind was free to adhere.

For this reason, God declares of Himself, "Vengeance is Mine, I will repay." The payment due to violations of His will, that is sin, is made very clear in Scripture. Paul wrote, "the wages of sin is death" (Rom. 6:23). There is a necessity that is demanded from sin and that necessity is death. All men, due to the fact that they have violated God's will, "for all have sinned and fall short of the glory of God" (Rom. 3:23), are thus subject to the punishment due them which is death, spiritually, physically, and eschatologically.

However, as we noted earlier, God had determined based on His own self-determination to save some who were rightfully condemned to death. But how could such be accomplished? To simply ignore or forgive their violation of His will would be the ultimate denial of His own nature. To dismiss the charges against a person who has committed a crime and broken the law is itself a crime. Not only this, but in God's case it would be a violation of His will. This is even evident in the Old Testament Law. The Law, as noted earlier, was a reflection of the will of God, which is itself a manifestation of God's nature. Part of the Law was the practice of recompense for those who violated it (Deut. 27:26; 30:15-20). Even unsaved man recognizes that violation demands punishment.

The answer to this dilemma is answered in the atonement being both substitutionary and vicarious. It is the fact that Christ's sacrifice is both substitutionary and vicarious that makes it possible for rightfully condemned sinners to be saved. Christ's sacrifice is substitutionary because God has graciously allowed Christ, who was not eligible to be punished due to His perfect life, to stand in the place of the sinner, who was rightly condemned and therefore to be punished. The carrying out of this gracious allowance we call vicarious. Vicarious in that Christ was actually punished in the stead of the sinner, He suffered a punishment that was not due Him, so that the sinner would not have to suffer the prescribed wage of his violation. The believer's guilt and sin was imputed to Christ and then punished in Christ, as the sinner's substitute.

This allowance and its carrying out is referred to by Paul in the following manner, "For you know the grace of our Lord Jesus Christ, that though He was rich, yet for your sake, He became poor, that you through His poverty might become rich" (2 Cor. 8:9). Peter puts it more simply than that. He sums it up in five words, "the just for the unjust." Truly indeed, He loved us.

Because Christ's atonement was both substitutionary and vicarious, it also accomplished reconciliation. Jesus did not die to make a relationship with God possible, He died in order to effect or cause such a relationship. You will remember that after Adam's fall that man hid himself from the presence of God. The relationship had changed as Genesis 3:8 makes clear. A one time open, forthright relationship turned into one of hiddenness and concealment. The two parties who were at one time at peace were now at war. Hostilities had broken out.

Paul summarizes the human side of this war as unsaved man being "hostile toward God" (Rom. 8:7; cf. Jam. 4:4). The divine side is described as the "wrath of God" (Rom. 1:18; 2:5-6; 3:3-6). A reconciliation was needed if the situation was going to be restored to its original peace. J. I. Packer in *Concise Theology* explains the situation as follows, "Reconciliation of the warring parties is needed, but this can occur only if God's wrath is somehow absorbed and quenched and man's anti-God heart, which motivates his anti-God life, is somehow changed."[17] Into this antagonistic situation stepped Christ, the Mediator. However, the amazing thing about His entrance is that it was initiated by the very One who was offended and wrathful towards those who were opposed to Him. That is nothing but grace in action. Grace would accomplish and bring about a reconciliation of the warring parties.

Christ, the Mediator, brought the two parties together by clearing away the guilt and sin of man and by such allowing God to express His love actively towards the transgressors of His will He had chosen in pardon and blessing. This was accomplished by expiating their guilt through the judgment due them being satisfied by Christ's substitutionary and vicarious sacrifice. But not just expiating the sinner's guilt through rightful punishment and thereby clearing it away, but also making God propitious towards those He had chosen.

Christ's sacrifice was propitious in reference to God, it meant that His love for us could now be exercised on our behalf to re-institute a positive relationship by pardoning and blessing the transgressor. With our guilt expiated or satisfied, our heinousness to Him being removed, God was now free to initiate our reconciliation to Him, through drawing us to Himself and granting us the faith to believe, which is propitiation. Truly indeed, He loved us.

For expiation and propitiation to take place and thus reconciliation to happen, then satisfaction must be a reality. Christ's death and the atonement it accomplished was also satisfactory. God must have accepted what Christ sought to accomplish in His death for its intended ends to take place. If God had simply left Christ in the grave, we would have no idea as to whether or not His work was approved by Him. That is the significance of the resurrection.

If Christ had simply lived and died two things would have been true: 1) He would be no different than any other self-proclaimed Messiah who lived and died during this time period; and 2) that which He indicated was the significance of His death, to ransom many (Mk. 10:45), would have been a false claim. But, God raised Him validating His life, His work, and His message. Peter summarizes all of this well when he writes in 1 Peter 3:18, "For Christ also died for sins once for all, the just for the unjust, in order that He might bring us to God, having been put to death in the flesh, but made alive in the spirit."

In a brief summary, this is the atonement: Christ's literal, final, and plenary substitutionary death for sin, for the condemned sinner, so that He might reconcile the sinner to God. On the cross, God imputed our sin and guilt to Christ and punished it in Christ. By doing so, His justice was maintained, while providing a way for sinners to be saved. This would be accomplished by imputing Christ's righteousness to the believing sinner. By doing that, He could accomplish the justifying of the sinner He desired. Or as Paul put it at the end of Romans 3:26, "that He might be just and the justifier of the one who has faith in Jesus." All evangelicals claim these things regarding the death of Christ.

The Particular Nature of Christ's Atonement

Defended

This is a unified evangelical position. We defer, however, on the objects of this atoning work of Christ.

First, let us understand where the disagreement lays. It is not in the sufficiency of Jesus' death. In other words, everyone who is truly a Christian on both sides of the fence believe that the death of Christ was more than a moral picture of love, more than an example of what we should do, more than a means of God maintaining His law, it was sufficient to place everyone in heaven. If that was God's will, nothing different would have to have been done. Jesus is the Godman, His death could have had the limitless effect of placing every single human being who ever lived or ever would live into heaven. No problem. Everyone believes that.

The question is this, was this the design of the atonement? In other words, when the atonement was planned, did God design it to pay the price for every human being's sin? To that question we answer no. Again, as noted earlier, no one questions the limitless sufficiency of the atonement, but rather we are focused here on whether the design and intent was limitless.

But let me say this before moving on. Both sides of this position limit the atonement in some way. Either you limit it on the front end or you limit it on the back end, but you do limit it. Our side says that the atonement was designed to atone for those God chose to save, while the other side says only those who believe have the atonement applied for them, but the design of the atonement was to pay for all human beings, even those who were not elected. Both sides limit the impact of the atonement. The atonement must be limited, or else you end up with universalism. The focal point of the debate centers around the inclusive language of some Bible passages. Just a few will be presented here with the debated language highlighted:

"The next day he saw Jesus coming to him, and said, "Behold, the Lamb of God who takes away the sin of **the world**!"

John 1:29

"For God so loved **the world**, that He gave His only begotten Son, that **whoever** believes in Him should not perish, but have eternal life. For God did not send the Son into the world to judge the world, but that **the world** should be saved through Him."

John 3:16-17

"And many more believed because of His word; and they were saying to the woman, "It is no longer because of what you said that we believe, for we have heard for ourselves and know that this One is indeed the Savior of **the world**."

John 4:41-42

"For the love of Christ controls us, having concluded this, that one died **for all**, therefore all died."

2 Corinthians 5:14

"For there is one God, *and* one mediator also between God and men, *the* man Christ Jesus, who gave Himself as a ransom **for all**, the testimony *borne* at the proper time."

1 Timothy 2:5-6

"But we do see Him who has been made for a little while lower than the angels, namely, Jesus, because of the suffering of death crowned with glory and honor, that by the grace of God He might taste death **for everyone**."

Hebrews 2:9

In these five examples, the work of Christ looks to be presented in a manner in which one would seem to have to view the atonement as unlimited, rather than limited. But are these verses only to be understood in this way? These verses when studied closer yield quite a different conclusion. What we will see is that the context of the statement determines the meaning of the word in that context. Looking at a few of these will give us an example of this particular fact.

In John 3:16-17, Jesus was continuing His conversation with a man named Nicodemus, a religious leader of his day (Jn. 3:1). Jesus had just spoken of the nature of the new birth (3:3-8) and the source of the new birth (3:9-15). Beginning in the sixteenth verse Jesus spoke to Nicodemus regarding His role in the new birth (3:16-21).

After stating God's love for the world, typified by His sending Christ to die, in order to provide salvation for whoever would believe, Jesus made a statement in the next verse which more closely defined the extent of the world spoken in 3:16. He says that He came that the world "should be saved through Him." If the purpose in His coming was that the whole world would be saved, He did not accomplish that purpose of God for which He was sent or else the whole world would be saved (see 3:18-21).

So, world must be other than every single human being in the world. A better understanding would be "the world" in the sense of human beings from every people, race, and walk of life. This is particularly appropriate given the example of the new birth found in the next chapter (4:1-42). The new birth was illustrated in the Samaritans, hated enemies of the Jews, who thought they were outside of God's program. Just the opposite was true, Jesus said salvation is for all types of people.

A similar conclusion is necessary from 2 Corinthians 5:14 as well, in which it seems to say that as a consequence of Christ's death, all of mankind died. Or in other words, all of mankind died with Christ. However, the implications of this would mean that all men are saved, which would lead one to conclude that universalism was true, not the Scriptures. This is because of Paul's statements in Romans 6. In this passage, he explains what identification with Christ's death does for a person,

> Therefore we have been buried with Him through baptism into death, in order that as Christ was raised from the dead through the glory of the Father, so we too might walk in newness of life. For if we have become united with Him in the likeness of His death, certainly we shall be also in the likeness of His resurrection, knowing this, that our old self was crucified with Him, that our body of sin might be done away with, that we should no longer be slaves to sin; for he who has died is freed from sin.
>
> Romans 6:4-7

Although baptism was not mentioned in 2 Corinthians, it was presented by Paul as the means by which a person was identified with Christ's death, which was his point in 2 Corinthians.

Another strong illustration can be found in Romans 10:9-13. In a span of these five verses Paul used the term "whoever" twice to demonstrate the scope of those to whom the gospel is directed (11, 13). One could therefore conclude that the atonement was to supply the possibility of salvation for any and everyone. However, in 10:12, Paul makes it clear what he and the Scriptures mean by "whoever," "For there is no distinction between Jew and Greek; for the same *Lord* is Lord of all, abounding in riches for all who call upon Him." Paul's meaning for his inclusive language is all types of people, rather than potentially all people.

Finally, in this regard, the very same reality is manifested in Hebrews 2:9. Hebrews 2:9 says, "But we do see Him who has been made for a little while lower than the angels, namely, Jesus, because of the suffering of death crowned with glory and honor, that by the grace of God He might taste death for everyone." It is impossible that "everyone" could mean here every human being for the author of Hebrews clearly limited it in the following verses, 2:10-13, where he labels the everyone as "many sons," "those who are sanctified," "brethren," and "the children whom God has given *to Christ*."

The author of Hebrews later used the same Greek word translated "everyone" to mean all of God's people, not all human beings (8:11; 12:8). It is clear from these passages, that words like everyone, all, and world are defined by the context, not by meanings imposed upon the text of Scripture by our human reasoning. So, it is important that one understand the context from which the passage is drawn before conclusions can be made regarding the extent of the meaning of the term "whole" or "all." To this may be added several other important proofs, regarding the limited nature of the atonement.

Expounded

Proof 1:   The Atonement is for the Elect

First, it is important to recognize that a great number of Scripture passages could be brought forward to demonstrate the position that the atonement is limited to just the church. In speaking to the elders of Ephesus when he left that region of Asia Minor, Paul made the following statement, "Be on guard for yourselves and for all the flock, among which the Holy Spirit has made you overseers, to shepherd the church of God which He purchased with His own blood" (Ac. 20:28). In this verse, the church was said to be that for which a price was paid.

Another passage which mentions Christ's work in reference to the church is that of Ephesians 5 in which Paul was discussing the relationship of the husband and wife mirroring the relationship of Christ and the church. Paul indicated of Christ "that He might present to Himself the church in all her glory, having no spot or wrinkle or any such thing; but that she should be holy and blameless" (5:27).

An even more pointed passage is found in the Gospel of John when Christ talks to the religious leaders regarding His sheep. Christ's words are specific, "But he who enters by the door is a shepherd of the sheep. To him the doorkeeper opens, and the sheep hear his voice and he calls his own sheep by name and leads them out . . . I am the good shepherd; the good shepherd lays down His life for the sheep" (Jn. 10:2-3, 11).

In each of these passages it is noted that the object of the atonement is the church or the individual believer, not the broadened focus of the world or all, as with which the previous passages dealt. That being the case, it must first be recognized that verses can be presented which establish a limited object for the atonement.

Proof 2: The Atonement is for All Types of Men

The next principle which must be realized is the dynamic nature of the meaning of "whole" and "all" in man's language. Both of these terms adapt to the nature of the context in which they are mentioned. For example, someone may ask the question, "who ate all of the rice" and mean "who ate all of the rice that was left in the container in the refrigerator." All in that context does not mean all the rice which was originally cooked, all the rice in the house, all the rice in the store. It simply means all the rice that remained.

Such usages of this term also appear in the biblical text. Take for instance Luke 2:1 which in the King James says, "And it came to pass in those days, that there went out a decree from Caesar Augustus, that all the world should be taxed." All the world here refers to all of the Roman Empire, not the entire inhabited world, because some of the world lay outside the boundaries of this proclamation. So all the world here is used to refer to a smaller group of people which comprised the Roman Empire.

Another illustration of this figure of speech is found in Mark 1:5. In speaking of the ministry of John the Baptist it says, "And all the country of Judea was going out to him, and all the people of Jerusalem; and they were being baptized by him in the Jordan River, confessing their sins." Are we to believe that every single man, woman and child in Judea and Jerusalem came out to hear John and was baptized? The rejection of John's ministry and Christ's seems to argue against that point. Also, the logistics of a whole region coming out to hear him seems near impossible. A better way of seeing the use of all, here, is the meaning of "many" or a "great number" of people.

Proof 3: The Meaning of the Atonement is Determined by the Context

Another principle that must be kept in mind while trying to understand the meaning of those passages dealing with the atonement, is the purpose of the passage or saying. One must understand whether or not the passage focuses upon the group of people from which the individual believer is being called, or towards believer's themselves. This is very important. The reason that this is important is based on several facts. First, although God has chosen certain individuals to be saved, they do not know who they are prior to their salvation. Second, other believers do not know who is chosen and who is not before they evangelize them. God is the only person who knows who they are.

Third, God has ordained the means by which the elect will become believers, which the Bible indicates is hearing and believing in the gospel (Rom. 10:1-21). With these three facts in mind, the purpose of the passage becomes crucial as to why certain inclusive language may be used.

Inclusive language would be used in contexts and in situations in which the boundaries of the gospel are being communicated. The gospel is to be presented to all people because no one knows who upon hearing would believe and who upon hearing would reject. That being the case, one would expect that inclusive rather than exclusive language would be used to present the gospel, since any one of the people being referred to may be one that God has chosen. What this shows is that inclusive language, on its own merit alone, cannot be used to prove that the atonement is unlimited, since it may simply be the outcome of a particular purpose of the passage.

Examples of this phenomena can be found in the book of Acts. The general appeal to believe was found at the end of the apostles' gospel preaching, as in the case of both Peter and Paul. Acts 10:43 climaxed Peter's gospel presentation to Cornelius' house. It said, "Of Him all the prophets bear witness that through His name everyone who believes in Him receives forgiveness of sins." This passage exhibits characteristics of both the previous principle as well as the one being discussed in this paragraph. The previous principle was that Peter was giving the gospel to Gentiles, which he was just realizing were included in God's salvation plan on equal terms (Ac. 10:34-35). The principle being discussed in this paragraph is that it was part of a gospel message Peter gave without knowing who in the household was ordained to believe.

Another passage in Acts 13:39 in which Paul says, "and through Him everyone who believes is freed from all things, from which you could not be freed through the Law of Moses." As in the case with Peter, Paul does not know who in that group is to be saved, so he gives a general invitation in case any of the elect are there to hear and believe. However, after the people's response to the gospel, a theological statement was made by Luke describing what took place. It was identified earlier, but make note of it again, "And when the Gentiles heard this, they began rejoicing and glorifying the word of the Lord; and as many as had been appointed to eternal life believed" (Ac. 13:48).

Peter's and Paul's inclusive language cannot be used to teach that Christ died for everyone, because in these passages the gospel is being presented to a group of people from which some may be chosen and some may not. The chosen will believe and the damned will not.

Proof 4: The Atonement Actually Accomplished Making Atonement

Another point of confusion lies in the fact that people mistakenly think that the death of Christ was simply to make salvation possible. We believe, instead, that the death of Christ was not to make salvation possible, but rather it was to accomplish the full and complete payment for sin upon the cross, it was to actually effect reconciliation, and it was to accomplish salvation in those for whom it was offered.

John the Baptist indicated just this fact when he said of Christ in John 1:29, "Behold, the Lamb of God who takes away the sin of the world!" Notice he did not say makes the taking away of sin possible, but actually takes it away. The word "world," here, of course must be a reference to all types of people irrespective of race, Jew or Gentile, not every single, individual person.

The reason that this must be the case is because of the just nature of God. Even human beings recognize that one cannot be in peril for the same crime in two different legal trials. To be in legal peril for murder, to be found innocent in that case, and then to be placed in legal peril again for that same murder is recognized even in human legal systems as unjust. We, in America, refer to this as double jeopardy. For Christ to have accomplished the forgiveness of a person's sins and then for God to punish the person for that exact same sin forgiven by Christ on the cross would be double jeopardy.

The author of Hebrews made a similar point when he wrote, "For by one offering He has perfected for all time those who are sanctified" (10:14). Notice not potentially, not possibly, but actually. The atonement actually affects sin's payment for those for whom it was offered. So, those whom Christ atoned for are those who Christ saves.

Proof 5:   The Atonement is Unlimited in Some Aspects

The final issue that must be taken into account when looking at the inclusive language of some of the biblical passages that deal with atonement is the different aspects of the atonement. The atonement made several provisions possible. Some of these were listed earlier in our discussion of the atonement.

One provision that it did make possible was the appeasement of God's wrath towards the sinner. This appeasement or propitiation has implications even for the unsaved world (1 Jn. 2:2). This is because God's wrath is being turned off towards the elect so that throughout human history He can bring in all those He has chosen. This means that due punishment is also held off of unbelievers, who would be deserving of that punishment.

God's active wrath in human history, which could have been immediate upon Adam's fall, has been forestalled while God has brought in His people. In this sense then, the atonement can be seen as applicable to the world while peculiar to the elect.

Summary

Therefore, it is apparent that the work of Jesus Christ on the cross was directed towards a certain group of people. That group of people is the elect, or His church. Passages in the Bible that speak with inclusive language only do so to communicate the context from which the elect are chosen, that is, the broader world of people.

Further, in some of the passages in which inclusive language is used the meaning should be understood to be the church or all those who would believe, based on the broader context of the passage. So, from the world of depraved men, God chose a few from the different races of mankind and provided the means for their salvation by sending His Son to die for them. The next doctrine of grace is that of irresistible grace, to which we now turn.

The Doctrine
of Irresistible Grace

It has already been noted that the means God has ordained to bring people to Himself is the hearing and believing of the gospel (Rom. 10). It has also been noted that in giving the gospel message inclusive language is used so as to address the elect in the context from which they will be coming. But how do the elect, for whom Christ has died, believe and thereby come out from amidst the masses of humanity?

This is where the doctrine of irresistible grace fits into the plan of God. Reformed believers hold that men are brought to saving knowledge of Jesus Christ through God's work of irresistible grace. Irresistible grace is that work of God whereby He unfailingly draws to Himself those to whom He has determined beforehand to extend His loving kindness, ultimately resulting in their salvation.

Proofs from Scripture

Several biblical passages articulate the idea of God's unfailing grace drawing those who are His chosen ones. 2 Thessalonians 2:13-14 provides a good stepping stone to examining some of these key passages and the ideas they communicate. In the second half of 2:13, Paul laid out the exact methodology of God by which He implemented His plan of salvation, which included His elective will, in time. The entire statement reads as follows,

> But we should always give thanks to God for you, brethren beloved by the Lord, because God has chosen you from the beginning for salvation through sanctification by the Spirit and faith in the truth. And it was for this He called you through our gospel, that you may gain the glory of our Lord Jesus Christ.

This statement finds its origin in Paul's intent to encourage the Thessalonians regarding their spiritual identity, which had been shaken according to his comments at the beginning of this chapter. There he laid out the deception that false teachers had tried to perpetrate upon them.

So, Paul began this statement with an acknowledgment of his and the entire mission team's thankfulness for them. This thankfulness, Paul indicated, was the consequence of or grew out of their spiritual identity. What was that spiritual identity? They were "beloved." Paul's confidence in the Thessalonians' position or status before God was not ultimately grounded for Paul in them, but rather in God. That is, in their election by God. Paul stated, "because God has chosen you from the beginning for salvation." Within this statement Paul identified the elective love of God for them as the ground of his confidence.

In describing this elective love of God, Paul noted that it was accomplished "through sanctification by the Spirit and faith in the truth." Here Paul communicated that the election of God is worked out irresistibly/sovereignly through the work of the Holy Spirit and the irresistible working of Faith.

The Irresistible Work of the Holy Spirit

The word "sanctification" is a term that believers are used to reading and seeing in the New Testament, in its various forms, sanctified, sanctify, etcetera. This term is often contrasted by Paul with such negative ideas as impurity, sexual immorality, lustful passion, transgressing one's brother, and the rejection of God. It is linked with the positive ideas of righteousness, redemption, honor, faith, love, and self-restraint. It actually comes from a word that has as its underlying concept, *holy*.

Holiness speaks to the issue of consecration and or purification. When someone consecrated something, they dedicated it or set it aside for a specific use. The use with which Scripture was concerned, of course, was the use of God. Purification was tied to this concept because for something to be placed in a sphere to be used by God, it needed to be purified. Purified from that which made it impure or from its baseness because it was man's or used by man.

When believers think of sanctification their mind usually goes to the spiritual reality that God accomplishes in the life of the saved sinner, whereby He progressively frees them from the power of sin that remains in their flesh after salvation. In this regard, sanctification is inseparably linked to justification. However, in all actuality, there are four uses to this idea in the New Testament.

The first of the three, positional sanctification, is synonymous with salvation and is the means whereby believers are actually set aside for God (1 Cor. 1:2; 6:11). Then there is practical or progressive sanctification whereby once saved believers are freed from the power of sin (1 Thess. 5:23). The third, prospective sanctification, is synonymous with glorification and is the means whereby believers are set aside from the very presence of sin through our final transformation (Eph. 5:26-27).

However, there is a fourth usage of this idea, a usage which is being communicated by the apostle Paul here in 2 Thessalonians 2:13. This is preparational sanctification. This type of sanctification precedes positional sanctification, that is salvation proper, and prepares the sinner for salvation. That this is the case can be seen by the fact that "faith in the truth" is what follows it, which is a reference to the exercise of faith in the gospel, the immediate cause of salvation.

Of course, we looked at this same idea earlier when we examined 1 Peter 1:2, which described God's choice or election of the believer, "according to the foreknowledge of God the Father, by the sanctifying work of the Spirit, that you may obey Jesus Christ and be sprinkled with His blood: May grace and peace be yours in fullest measure." We noted that in Peter's statement the sanctification being addressed preceded the obeying of Jesus to be sprinkled with His blood, which is also a reference to salvation.

So, it is with the experience of this preparational sanctification of the Holy Spirit that God's effectual grace is expressed. The Spirit's preparational sanctification begins with His work of conviction. The convicting work of the Holy Spirit is that act of the Holy Spirit whereby He accomplishes three things.

According to John 16:8-11, He convinces the unbeliever of their sin, typified by their unbelief in Christ, He convinces them of Christ's right standing before God, typified by God's acceptance of Jesus back to heaven, and He convinces them of their ensuing judgment, typified in the judgment of the devil himself (cf. Mt. 25:41).

The conviction of the Holy Spirit does not necessarily lead to salvation and does not do more than weigh negatively upon the conscious unless linked to the effectual drawing of God.

However, for those who are to be saved, the salvation process in their life will be initiated with conviction. Speaking of this threefold process, J. I. Packer wrote the following words, "This threefold conviction is still God's means of making sin repulsive and Christ adorable in the eyes of persons who previously loved sin and cared nothing for the divine Savior."[18] So conviction begins the process. It is part of the Spirit's preliminary work in the heart of the person who will eventually receive Christ as their Savior. This process works to lay the groundwork for convincing the unbeliever of the truth regarding Christ and his own wretchedness in light of that truth. In this state of Spirit produced conviction, that sinner may despair over who he is and cower before the fury of a righteously indignant God. However, due to his lingering depravity, he cannot make any movement to be rescued from that condition and in fact foolishly resists it.

From conviction the sinner is moved to God by the Spirit's work of drawing. The unbeliever so convicted is then drawn by the Holy Spirit to God's goal, which is his salvation. He points the sinner towards Christ, as the only source of help for his plight and makes Christ most attractive. John 6 explains how this takes place and its effectual or irresistible nature.

This chapter begins with the feeding of the five thousand, followed by the miracle of Jesus walking on the water (6:1-25). The miracle of the feeding spawned a reaction in those who experienced it of wanting more of the same from Jesus. They followed Him not for spiritual reasons, but for physical ones, as Jesus Himself noted, "Jesus answered them and said, 'Truly, truly, I say to you, you seek Me, not because you saw signs, but because you ate of the loaves, and were filled'" (6:26). Although they vehemently denied this, as Jesus conversed with them in the following verses, it became clear that they were far from coming to Him for spiritual purposes. As a result they began to grumble at His words (6:41).

Why were they resistant to the truth about who Christ truly was and the Father's relationship to Him? Jesus' answer was not what most people expect. Was it simply because they were stubborn or confused? Absolutely not, it had as much to do with the Father as with them. Earlier He had told them, "All that the Father gives Me shall come to Me, and the one who comes to Me I will certainly not cast out" (6:37). Now Jesus stated, "Do not grumble among yourselves. No one can come to Me, unless the Father who sent Me draws him; and I will raise him up on the last day" (Jn. 6:43-44).

The reason was not because they did not know the gospel nor because they did not have their questions answered. Rather the reason that they did not come to Christ was they were, negatively speaking, spiritually unable, and because of the fact that, positively speaking, they were not drawn by God. Without such a drawing, salvation was impossible, for sinful inability can only be overcome by irresistible and effectual movement of the divine on the heart.

Some people incorrectly appeal to John 12:32 to disprove this conclusion, but far from it disproving it, it fits into the basic worldview communicated by it. It is concluded by some that John 12:32 indicates that all men will be drawn to Christ. What they fail to understand is that such an interpretation of that passage results logically in universalism. How? Christ indicated in John 6:44 that those who come to Christ are those who are drawn to Him by the Father. If every human being is drawn to Christ, then every human being will eventually be saved. Nowhere do we read in the Bible where this drawing spoken of by Christ in John 6:44 is resistible.

It is better to take John 12:32 in its context and not to interpret it against its context. The context of Jesus' statement begins with the events of 12:20-26, where a group of Gentiles wanted to have a private meeting with Jesus, which lead Christ into a series of statements about His death and salvation. The point of Jesus' statement in 12:32 when Jesus says "all men" was all types of men, Jew or Gentile, any race without bias and without prejudice. This affirms, not works against, the point being made in John 6.

Only those drawn by the Father can come to Christ. It is important to note that the end point of the drawing of God is being raised "up on the last day." There is a natural progression when someone is brought to faith in Christ. This is a particularly important passage because Christ was explaining the rejection by those who were having His role on the earth explained to them. Christ's explanation of mankind's rejection of Him is not that they do not believe, but rather that they do not believe because they were not given to Him by the Father and, thus, are not drawn by God.

Now, where is the Spirit here? Well, make note of the fact that Jesus used the same Greek term in John 12:32 to describe His drawing of people to Himself. But rather than the Father doing it, it is Him doing it. This passage is important because one needs to see that this drawing work is Trinitarian in its nature. That which is done by the

The Doctrine of Irresistible Grace

Trinity is planned or framed by the Father, is provided for by the Son, and is executed by the Spirit. All three members of the Godhead have a hand in it.

These ideas regarding the workings of the Godhead with the world and those in the world are illustrated throughout the Bible. One illustration is found in the relationship of the Godhead in the accomplishment of the creation. The creation itself as a fact is attributed to the Father (Gen. 1:1; Mk. 10:6). The creation itself, although attributed to the Father, was actually carried out through the Son, who spoke the plan forth, as the Divine Word of God (Gen. 1; Jn. 1:1-3; Heb. 1:1-2). Finally, the Father's plan to create for which Christ provided, was done by the direct workings of the Holy Spirit (Gen. 1:2).

Now, even though these things are the case, so perfect is the working of the Godhead in all that He does, and so thoroughly unified are those workings, that acts carried out by one member are attributed to others. So, for example, although Jesus is the Savior, the Father can also bear that title (cf. 1 Tim. 1:1). After all, was it not the Father's plan for salvation for which the Son made adequate provision?

Also, although it is the Father's will that is paramount in the operations of the Trinity, the Holy Spirit can be said to grant gifts according to His own will (cf. 1 Cor. 12:11). So, in the Godhead each person of the Trinity carries out certain operations in perfect symmetry with the others. From this we can conclude that it is the Holy Spirit's job to take the plan of the Father and the provision of the Son, and make it effective in the lives of those whom He has chosen for salvation.

So, doctrinally, the Spirit of God would be the member of the Godhead who executed the specific task of working on the human heart to irresistibly draw the sinner to Christ. This is in perfect accord with the Holy Scriptures. Christ Himself noted that not only would the Spirit of God be His living presence on the earth and in the believer (Jn. 14:16-18), He would also teach of Christ and disclose of Christ (14:26; 16:13-15). Christ would be His focus. Should it not be expected that He would act in Christ's stead and point and draw all types of men unto Him, as conviction illustrates?

In concert with this drawing is the teaching of the sinner. God does not work upon the person in such a way as to avoid or circumvent the human mind. He rather works within the capacities and faculties of mankind.

In this regard return once again to John 6. John 6:44 should not be separated from the next verse, which is key to understanding what this divinely initiated drawing entails. Jesus continued, "It is written in the prophets, 'And they shall all be taught of God.' Everyone who has heard and learned from the Father, comes to Me" (6:45).

In this verse, Jesus referred to Isaiah 54:13 as a proof text that being "taught of God" is a necessary aspect to His drawing of those whom He has chosen unto Christ, as Jesus taught earlier in 6:37. This being "taught of God," is a necessary precursor to salvation because it involves hearing and learning from the Father, which is said to precede coming to Christ. In other words, Jesus is here referring to a work of God in the sinner previous to salvation that is related to leading or drawing him to Christ for salvation.

This passage is important for our understanding of our subject matter in this chapter because it indicates that there is a divinely produced learning that precedes salvation, which is successfully accomplished in all who become believers and therefore is universal to all Christians. How so? Because Jesus indicated that it is only those who have experienced it who come to Him. Again, this act would be accomplished in the sinner by the Spirit. He operates on behalf of the Trinity effecting or bringing about the work of the Trinity.

So then, through the working of the Holy Spirit sovereignly and irresistibly convicting, drawing, and teaching the sinner, He prepares the sinner to finally exercise faith. Although unsaved, he is convinced of his impending judgment and despairs that if left in his condition, he will surely perish. Although unsaved, he is brought to an awareness of his need to escape, but knows not what to do to experience such. Although unsaved, he finds himself peculiarly influenced towards a person named Jesus Christ, in spite of his previous hateful disposition towards Him and his present resistance. Then at the right moment, at God's moment, the Spirit regenerates the convinced, drawn, and taught sinner and grants them faith and they believe. Which is Paul's final point in this verse.

The Irresistible Working of Faith

Paul concluded the thought with the following statement "and faith in the truth." The idea of "the truth" in this particular context which is dealing with salvation, speaks to not the doctrine of the Christian faith, but here it is focused upon the message of truth, that is the gospel. The labeling of the message that ushers individuals into the church being described simply as "the truth" finds its justification in the nature of the church itself.

Paul described the church as the "pillar and support of the truth" (1 Tim. 3:15). This indicated that the manifestation of the truth within the world is dependent upon the church. Further, the Leader or Head of the church to whom the members of the church pledge their undying allegiance referred to Himself as not only the Way and the Life, but also the Truth (Jn. 14:6). Is it surprising, then, that the message a person hears and in which they believe to become a member of this church, the pillar and support of the truth, led by a person referred to as the Truth, is itself described as the message of truth? Paul wrote, "In Him, you also, after listening to the message of truth, the gospel of your salvation—having also believed, you were sealed in Him with the Holy Spirit of promise" (Eph. 1:13; cf. Col. 1:5; 2 Thess. 2:10; Jam. 1:18).

To have faith in this message, is to believe or trust what it says to be true and entrust yourself to it. Let me explain. When discussing the issue of faith one's habit is to immediately turn to Hebrews 11:1, which describes faith as follows, "Now faith is the assurance of things hoped for, the conviction of things not seen." But other Scriptures should also leave their mark on the believer's understanding of what faith means.

For example, one should learn from Romans 3:27-28 that faith is something that stands in stark and absolute contrast to both works and the Law for Paul wrote, "Where then is boasting? It is excluded. By what kind of law? Of works? No, but by a law of faith. For we maintain that a man is justified by faith apart from works of the Law." Works and Law are not compatible as means with the means of faith (cf. Gal. 3:11-12).

One should also note from the book of Romans that faith is expressed through believing in God and thus trusting Him. This is evident by Paul's use of Abraham as an example of faith. Notice his words in Romans 4:1-5,

> What then shall we say that Abraham, our forefather according to the flesh, has found? For if Abraham was justified by works, he has something to boast about; but not before God. For what does the Scripture say? "And Abraham believed God, and it was reckoned to him as righteousness." Now to the one who works, his wage is not reckoned as a favor, but as what is due. But to the one who does not work, but believes in Him who justifies the ungodly, his faith is reckoned as righteousness.

All sinners who would be saints, must exercise this faith by the act of believing. Again, Ephesians 1:13 stated this very fact, "In Him, you also, after listening to the message of truth, the gospel of your salvation—having also believed, you were sealed in Him with the Holy Spirit of promise."

We might look at faith then as the human response to the message of the truth, that is the gospel, whereby the sinner, having relinquished his claims to his own life and repented of his sin, believes the message of truth that the resurrected Lord Jesus Christ is the only means to salvation from sin and judgment and a proper relationship with God;

and trusts in God alone that this is indeed the case. Without such exercise of faith it is impossible for a person to receive Christ and to be saved.

This faith is a gift of God that is given in concert with the regeneration that precedes conversion, which was stated at the conclusion of the previous section. This sequence is clearly laid out to the believer in Ephesians 2. You will notice that before Paul indicates that the believer is saved by grace through faith, he first indicated in 2:4-5, "But God, being rich in mercy, because of His great love with which He loved us, even when we were dead in our transgressions, made us alive together with Christ (by grace you have been saved)." Since a person can not initiate or effect their own resurrection, this is the unilateral work of God in the life of the believer, described in the previous section of this chapter.

It is this and being seated with Christ, which Paul mentioned in the following verses (2:6-7), that Paul in 2:8 labels as being saved by grace through faith. And it is this faith that Paul indicated was given as a gift to the sinner whom God has chosen to be a saint. Included with this gift of faith was the gift of repentance, the flip side of faith (cf. Ac. 5:31; 11:18; 20:21; 2 Tim. 2:25). God gives the sinner He has chosen the capacity to be able to turn from his sin in repentance. Once regenerated and gifted with repentance and faith, the convicted, drawn, taught, and now regenerated sinner, turns from their sin and believes on God with the faith that is given to him, and he is converted.

It is for this reason that Paul boldly affirms in Romans 10:17 that, "faith comes from hearing, and hearing by the word of Christ." This is why it is so important that believers share their faith with those whom they come across in their lives. God uses the proclamation of the gospel to all they meet to grant repentance and faith to His elect, in order to save those whom He has chosen. It is God's will that determines who is saved. Therefore, believers have no right to determine with whom they will share the message of truth, the gospel.

Proofs from the Doctrines Grace

Before summarizing our discussion of irresistible grace, it is important to recognize that the relationship of the other doctrines to it, also serve to demonstrate its validity. Total depravity would mandate that God irresistibly draw the person to Himself, since in and of themselves, they cannot come to Him.

Also, unconditional election lends itself to irresistible grace in that by unfailingly drawing those whom He has chosen, God guarantees the salvation of the elect.

Further, the doctrine of limited atonement also matches with the doctrine of irresistible grace. God's directing of the aspects of the atonement that deal with salvation to those whom He has chosen, would mean that He would see to it that it was definitively applied to them.

Irresistible Grace Applied

For the reformed person, salvation is of the Lord. It was planned by God and it is applied by God. Man's only duty is to respond to it aright, that is to exercise the faith that he has been given. It is important to recognize at this juncture, just how irresistible grace is applied to God's chosen ones. The question here is "Is the believer converted and then regenerated, or regenerated and then converted?" In other words, does belief precede the new birth or follow it?

To fully understand the answer to this question, one must grapple with the fact that there are two spheres of operation or perspectives on life. One is man's plane, which is bound by time and a sequence of events, and the other is God's plane, which is not bound by time and sequence, just God's own logical order. While the two planes do not contradict each other, they will vary because of a different orientation.

An illustration will make the point clear. In the mind of God, He is unaware of nor susceptible to any time sequence. He knows all the events of 2017 and all the years previous, and if He tarries, all the years future all at once. In other words, He knows all the events of Human history all at the same time. However, He is also aware of logical order, that is, that the events of 2014 will have preceded the events of 2015 in human history; again, because He planned it that way. Human beings, however, are only aware of things as they unfold in human history, one year after another. So God's plane of existence and man's plane of existence are totally different. These basic truths can be helpful in understanding the doctrine of irresistible grace.

In human terms, when salvation comes into a person's life, it comes with the sequence of believe and be saved. One believes the gospel message upon hearing it, repents, and is born again (Jn. 3:3, 16; Ac. 3:19; 26:20). This sequence matches with the proclamation of the gospel, which is the ordained means of bringing the elect to salvation. From God's vantage point, however, the sequence is much different. One is born again, and therefore believes. Again, this is apparent from the total depravity of man.

If man is totally depraved, then he does not possess the capabilities of believing the gospel once it is presented to him. As noted earlier in discussing the doctrine of total depravity, unsaved man is spiritually dead. Spiritually dead people cannot respond spiritually and believe. Unsaved man is also said to be blinded to the gospel (2 Cor. 4:3-4). Spiritually blind people cannot spiritually see in order to come when the gospel is presented to them. So, before they can believe, they must be made alive from their dead state and then made to see from their blind state. This is none other than being born again. Upon being born again, they then exercise faith, believe, and are converted.

Summary

So the doctrine of irresistible grace claims that God sovereignly and unfailingly draws to Himself those whom He has chosen to love. This effectual drawing is combined with an effectual call and the new birth, ending up in the one chosen believing the gospel and turning to God.

The Doctrine of the Perseverance of the Saints

With the doctrine of the perseverance of the saints, the doctrines of grace come to a climax. The focus of the doctrines of grace is the salvation of man, while the perseverance of the saints speaks to the assurance of the completion of that salvation process.

In speaking of the perseverance of the saints, Calvinists hold that it is the work of God in and through man, whereby all those who are truly saved will progressively and consistently respond to God's work and therefore always believe and trust in Christ, never falling away or failing to grasp that for which God called them, that is eternal life. This is a promise given by Christ, who gave His word saying, "Truly, truly, I say to you, he who hears My word, and believes Him who sent Me, has eternal life, and does not come into judgment, but has passed out of death into life" (Jn. 5:24).

One of the Greek terms that we translate "save" in the Bible meant to rescue from harm or danger. Why would God rescue people that He Himself could not in turn keep? Although some believe that this rescue, accomplished by God, can be lost by the one so saved, we deny such is possible. Instead we affirm along with the Holy Scriptures that the God who began the work described above has both the capacity and intent to finish it. To lose your salvation, one would have to pass back out of life into death, a total reversal of what defines the Christian in the first place (1 Jn. 3:14). He would have to die again spiritually speaking. He would have to undo what God did.

As you can see, one of the most precious doctrines of the Christian faith is the perseverance of the saints. It encapsulates the interaction between God and the believer that comes as a result of salvation. However, there are some passages that appear to allow for the idea of losing one's salvation. Although this is the case, upon closer examination, the proper interpretation of these passages yields support for the idea of perseverance.

For example, in John 15 Jesus spoke of two branches, one that produced no fruit and the second which produced fruit. On the surface it would appear that they both seemed to be saved. However, Jesus' statement that the disciples, minus Judas, were clean in 15:3 referred the reader back to John 13:5-11, which clearly pinpointed Judas as not being saved, although a part of the group. This indicated that the context of Jesus' statement was regarding those, who like Judas, only appear to be saved through their association with the people of God. Their lack of spiritual fruit, that is spiritual virtues, testify to their lack of spiritual life. This is made plain when Jesus stated, "If anyone does not abide in Me, he is thrown away as a branch, and dries up; and they gather them, and cast them into the fire, and they are burned" (15:6).

A similar reality is seen in Hebrews 6, which seems to indicate that individuals who have experienced spiritual life, that is being enlightened, tasted, and being made partakers, can fall away (6:4-6). The problem with this argument is that the situation is hypothetical, as the change in pronouns from "us" and "we" in 6:1-3 to "those" in 6:4-6 indicated.

Second, if this passage taught that you could lose your salvation, then it would also be impossible for them to be saved again, for the author wrote, "it is impossible to renew them again to repentance, since they again crucify to themselves the Son of God, and put Him to open shame" (6:6).

Third, the author goes on to explain himself in 6:7-8, as the word "For" indicated, giving an illustration of what he meant. It is clear from this illustration that those who appear to be saved but do not bring forth fruit witness to their lack of saving faith, and those who bear fruit, demonstrate their conversion.

So, let us take a closer look at this important doctrine and its encouragement to the believer. In examining this doctrine, a proper understanding of it can be gained through looking at it from man's vantage point and God's vantage point. As to the former, the believer is said to abide, and as to the latter, God keeps. First, let us look at God's keeping of the believer.

God Keeps the Believer

There is not a more reassuring biblical truth than that the believer is kept by God. This is to be expected, after all, it is God who has planned for the believer's salvation. Also, it was God who relinquished His Son to provide a way for that plan to be executed, and who sent His Holy Spirit to guide and direct the believer in his unsaved days to His Son Jesus Christ.

Further, at the most opportune time, God was the one who caused the believer to be born again, not because of anything the believer had done, not in a response to the believer's actions, but solely and completely upon His grace. Now, should one think that the God who did this, would not see to it that His work would be completed? The Bible clearly affirms that His grace maintains the believer for such a time as He is ready to complete that salvation. We will now investigate this truth.

John 10:27-30

The tenth chapter of John has already been a part of the study of the doctrines of grace. It can also be used here as well. In John 10, Jesus was discussing His role, position, and nature as the Good Shepherd. When a controversy arose regarding His deity (10:19-24), Jesus responded by testifying to why the controversy existed and what His true character really was (Jn. 10:25-30).

The controversy developed out of the fact that those who were having a problem with Him were those who were really not His sheep, (those who both knew Him and followed Him) (10:25-27). Jesus' response to this knowing and following of Him by His sheep was to "give eternal life to them, and they shall never perish" (10:28). Christ guaranteed His sheep with the completion of their salvation in heaven with Him.

One might wonder, "how could such be guaranteed to be accomplished?" This He established in the next clause, in which He stated, "no one shall snatch them out of My hand." The securing of the believer for eternal life happens because Christ holds His sheep in His hand. Obviously, Christ was not speaking of His physical hand, but was using hand, as the Bible so often does, as a representation of a person's power (Job 40:14; Ps. 17:7; 20:6; 110:1; Isa. 48:13; 50:2).

Therefore, eternal life was guaranteed to Jesus' sheep because God keeps them by His power. But Christ did not stop here. He went on to say, "My Father, who has given *them* to Me, is greater than all; and no one is able to snatch *them* out of the Father's hand" (10:29).

Not only are they in the hand of Christ, but they are also in the hand of God the Father. In other words, being kept by the power of Christ is the same as being kept by the power of the Father (10:30). The true believer, one of

Christ's sheep, is secure in their eternal destiny because they are kept and guarded by the power of God.

Romans 8:28-29

Romans 8 has already been used in reference to the irresistible grace of God, but can also be used to demonstrate God's keeping of the believer. As stated at that time, there is an unbreakable tie between God's predestinating, calling, and justifying of those whom He foreknew (8:29-30). But Paul finished 8:30 by noting that the ones who were justified are the same ones who "He also glorified."

This is interesting because glorification is a future event, that will take place when the believer is taken to heaven. However, the form of the word in the text is past tense. Paul was, therefore, representing the future event of glorification as a past event in the action of God.

So secure is the believer's future of taking place that God represents his future as a past accomplished fact. God guarantees that all those whom He justifies, He will glorify them to be with Him in heaven.

Ephesians 1:13-14

The first chapter of Ephesians is one of the richest sources of information and exhortation on both the origin and outworking of the Christian life. Paul, masterfully presented the believer's salvation as begun in eternity past with the planning of the trinity through the sacrifice of Christ for those who were to be saved. Ultimately this plan ended up in the application of this salvation to the believer in human history by the Holy Spirit. All of this takes place in only the first fourteen verses of the first chapter (1:3-14).

Throughout the passage the phrase "in Him" is repeated, which is a reference to Christ Himself. He is the undergirding foundation of the passage for 1:3 says, "Blessed *be* the God and Father of our Lord Jesus Christ, who has blessed us with every spiritual blessing in the heavenly *places* in Christ." The focal point of this passage in reference to the perseverance of the saints is found in the concluding two verses of his opening thought (1:13-14).

In these verses, Paul explains the Holy Spirit's role in the salvation process. He began 1:13 with Christ again, the foundation, in whom something special has occurred to the believer. This something took place after a certain event. That event was the combination of hearing and believing in the gospel, which we have already noticed is God's ordained means of the elect attaining the salvation He has planned for them.

After this took place, Paul indicated to the Ephesians that they "were sealed in Him with the Holy Spirit of promise." The idea of sealing something in biblical days was the idea of setting an official mark or stamp on something in order to identify the owner, the owner's guarantee of the contents, and the owner's authority over the item stamped. For the Christian, the Holy Spirit is God's special seal or identification and guarantee of that which is promised to him in Christ. The seal of Christ is upon the believer, placed there by the Holy Spirit.

Based on this, the Holy Spirit is said in the next verse to be "given as a pledge of our inheritance, with a view to the redemption of *God's own* possession, to the praise of His glory." The Holy Spirit who sealed the believer is also the one pledged to the believer. The idea of "pledge" was taken from the arena of finances and commerce and was compatible with the concept of "earnest money" or a "down payment." This spoke of a portion of the price of an object being given to the store keeper in order to set something aside. The rest of the money making up the full price would be given at a later date when the object was taken into the possession of the one purchasing it.

This rich idea was what was being communicated here by the apostle. The Holy Spirit is the believer's down payment given to him by God in lieu of the full dispensing of the believer's inheritance to him at the time of his final redemption (cf. Rom. 8:23). God will in the future give the believer all that He has planned for him. However, until that day, the Holy Spirit has been given to the Christian as a down payment of receiving of the future inheritance.

Now the implications of these two truths, the sealing of the Holy Spirit and the Holy Spirit being a pledge to the believer, are clear for the doctrine of perseverance of the saints. God keeps the believer from ultimate apostasy in that He has set His seal of identification upon him and has given His pledge of a future with Him, so He cannot allow him to fall away from his intended goal. That is, the ultimate and final salvation of his body and soul.

Philippians 1:6

The sixth verse of the first chapter of the book of Philippians contains an encouraging statement for the believer's often troubled and difficult life here on the earth. Paul told the believer's of Philippi, after thanking them for their joint participation with him and the rest of the missions team in the gospel, that he was "confident of this very thing, that He who began a good work in you will perfect it until the day of Christ Jesus." Paul was indicating to them that their work on his behalf (cf. 1:7; 4:10-20) has evidenced to him that God is truly at work in their lives.

With that being true, he is absolutely sure that God, the author of the good work in them, will perfect it. The term "perfect" meant to bring to completion, or to its final stage. God leaves no projects undone. Unlike man's feeble attempts to complete those things he starts, God, because of His omnipotence and sovereignty, can complete everything that He works on. Therefore, the believer cannot ultimately fail to attain the salvation into which he was called because God will finish what He has started in him.

1 Peter 1:3-5

1 Peter 1:1-2 has already been examined in reference to the doctrine of election, but now we will continue on and investigate the next three verses which are Peter's articulation of the outcome of being born again. Peter began with a doxology or statement of praise (1:3). He

urged his readers to recognize with him the blessedness of God. He then gave the reason why such should be the believer's response in the verses that follow, by explaining what was done for the believer by this God who is to be blessed.

God is the One who caused the believer to be born again, and such was done on the basis of His great mercy, as 1:2 indicates. It is important to note here that God is the ultimate cause of salvation, not the person being saved or anything that person has done. The position of Scripture is that salvation, whether it be physical or spiritual, is from the LORD (Ps. 3:8; Jn. 2:9). Peter then lists two things to which the believer was born again: 1) a living hope (1:3); and 2) an inheritance (1:4).

First, Peter indicated that the new birth of the believer was to a living hope. In other words, it was not a hope that was wrongly founded or informed. It was a hope that was true and sure. According to Peter, the believer has that hope through Christ's resurrection.

Many times in Scripture the believer's hope was linked with or tied to the resurrection of Christ or the subsequent outcome of that resurrection, His glorification or return (cf. 1 Pet. 13, 21). The believer's hope was in that which will be rendered to him at the return of Christ and it was gained for him by the work of Christ, both of which center upon the resurrection of the Lord (cf. Rom. 8:17-25).

How false and cruel God would be if He gave us something in which to hope, and then did not do that for which He produced the hope in us in the first place. Believers have not hoped in God in vain, but He will keep them to the point of their ultimate destination (1 Pet. 1:13, 21).

According to Peter the believer has also been born again to an inheritance. This inheritance was described using four terms. First, he noted that it was imperishable. The idea here is something that was not susceptible to decay, wear and thus destruction. By using this term, Peter communicated the idea of an alteration of something because of an internal change of its character. The believer's inheritance will not be altered by any internal deficit.

Second, the inheritance was called undefiled. The focal point of this term was that this inheritance can not be affected by contamination, stain or pollution. In other words, the alteration of a substance or a thing by way of some outside source denigrating it. The believer's inheritance will not be affected by any external forces.

Third, he said the believer's inheritance will not fade away. The idea here was of something which began in one state and through time gradually lost any luster, brilliance or shine it once had. Such fading may happen because of corruption, decay, use or lack of use. The primary focus, however, seemed to be the fading that would be based on time. However the Christian's inheritance, that which God has promised to him, will not suffer any such tapering, diminishing, or dulling. From the day it was promised to the day it is claimed, through to eternity it will not dim in any form or fashion.

Finally, Peter indicated that this inheritance has been set aside for the believer. He said it has been "reserved in heaven for you." The idea of reserve was to keep something for a specific purpose, much in the same way as a jailer would keep under lock and key those placed in his charge. So the believer's inheritance is right now being kept specifically and specially for him. If God is going to keep the believer's inheritance safe for him, there must be some way in which He plans to see to it that the believer and the believer's inheritance meet. Peter indicated such in the next verse.

Peter continued by indicating that the believer was being "protected by the power of God." The main idea was that of an army guarding a city. The city was man's soul, and the army was the power of God. The means by which this protection was executed was "through faith" Peter said. The purpose for which this protection was being carried out was "for a salvation ready to be revealed in the last time."

The believer was being preserved by God, because God must finally give to him that which He has promised to him. At the completion of his salvation the believer will take full possession of those marvelous things God set aside for him.

What was Peter saying? Peter indicated to his readers that God should, and must be, praised for what He has done in giving new birth based on His marvelous mercy to those He chose. That new birth has given them a true and real hope and an inheritance which can not be affected in anyway. God was keeping it for them, protecting them until He can finally give it to them in full.

Therefore, the Bible clearly indicates that God keeps the believer in order to give to him that which he has only begun to experience here on earth. God's purposes in this area, as in any other area of His plan, cannot be thwarted or changed. He will accomplish and complete that which He has begun to do in the Christian's life. But what is to be the believer's response to what God is working in his life? This will be explained in the following section.

The Believer Abides in Christ

God's role in the perseverance of the saints is to keep. The role of man in the process is to abide in Christ. The New Testament teaches that all those who are true believer's will persevere in remaining in Christ.

When someone trusts in Christ their character or makeup totally changes. Before they were saved, they were totally and absolutely under the control of the flesh. Their state was characterized by being spiritually dead, as stated in the discussion of the doctrine of total depravity (Eph. 2:1). Paul described this state as one in which the person conducted himself by the standards and directions of the world, by the directions of Satan, and by the lusts of his own flesh (Eph. 2:2-3).

At that time or in that state, God found us and regenerated us, or gave us new birth. This new birth encompassed God giving to the sinner a new inner man, one "which in *the likeness of* God has been created in righteousness and holiness of the truth" (Eph. 4:24). This new inner man displaced the old man the believer once was and "is being renewed to a true knowledge according to the image of the One who created him" (Col. 3:10).

Paul explained this process when he wrote, "knowing this, that our old self was crucified with *Him*, that our body of sin might be done away with, that we should no longer be slaves to sin, for he who has died is freed from sin" (Rom. 6:6-7). This means that sin is no longer the master of the believer. It no longer rules him as a tyrant and a task master, to make him do whatsoever it wills. For this reason, the believer is faced with the challenge of defeating sin in his body.

His inner man is new, but his outer man is still in need of change. He needs a new physical body (Rom. 8:23-25). His lack of it makes him cry out with the apostle Paul, "Wretched man that I am! Who will set me free from the body of this death" (Rom. 7:24). The answer to which is God Himself in Christ (1 Cor. 15:35-58).

So the believer's fight with sin is one he will win through Christ. The bondage to sin has been broken, therefore he can and does abide in Christ, that is, in an obedient state or pattern of life to Christ (1 Jn. 3:4-12). This obedient lifestyle is ongoing for the believer. This expectation is expressed in many different forms in the New Testament.

John 15:1-6

There exists a biblical mandate for abiding, which is found in John 15:1-6, and its broader context of John 15:1-11. This passage of scripture is found in what is referred to as the Upper Room Discourse. The Upper Room Discourse, which extends from John 13 through John 17, is Jesus' last extended teaching moment with His disciples before His crucifixion. In it we have the heart of Jesus' instruction for His disciples.

John 15:1-6 is one of the most difficult passages in the Bible to understand. As such a careful study of it will be needed if we are to properly understand and apply it. The difficulty lies in the fact that the branch (or person) that seems to be in Christ (15:2), but does not produce fruit is burned up (15:6). How does this align with eternal security? The first truth we must realize before we look at the passage is that the Bible clearly teaches that the Believer is eternally secure, as we have already seen. That is once a person is saved, He is always saved, or in other words, God completes what He finishes. This passage focuses upon man's responsibility of abiding.

The chapter opens up in 15:1 with Jesus giving the disciples the source of growth in the believer's life. Growth does not happen independent of the vine. When you cut a branch off from the vine it does not grow, it can not grow. Therefore, it is only in being properly connected to the vine that growth can take place.

It is also important to notice that even the producer or catalyst of the growth was not the branch, but the vinedresser who was God, the Father, who took responsibility for the branch's growth. Christ then contrasted two different branches, one bears fruit and the other does not (15:2). Since the difficulty was the one who does not bear fruit, we will leave this person until we reach 15:6, where his story picks up again.

It says that the one who bears fruit will be pruned for the purpose of bearing more fruit. Growth was not a one time thing in the believer's life. It was an ongoing process that God controls. Notice that God has the pruning shears, not the believer. God was the one who was to do the cutting, not the believer. God picks the time not the believer. Believers are pruned whether they like it or not.

The third verse in this passage claimed that the disciples were already clean. The word translated "clean" in this verse was from the same root word as that which is translated prunes in the previous verse. What Jesus was saying was that the disciples were in a state of being pruned.

This brings up the issue of Judas, however. Was he included in Jesus' words here? From Jesus' statement in John 13:6-11, it is clear that he was not. However, up to this point in the narrative, the disciples were still believing that he was included (Jn. 13:29-30). So when these statements were taken in light of the defection of Judas, they are properly understood as a statement of the identification of true believers with false believers, like Judas.

The true disciple is properly related to the vine and therefore bears fruit. John 15:3-4 is quite insistent about the source and means of growth. Jesus stated the source of growth quite emphatically, when He said "the branch cannot bear fruit of itself . . . apart from Me you can do nothing." The means of growth was abiding in Christ. No growth could take place outside of Christ and as such for growth to occur the believer must remain in Christ.

The non-fruit bearing branch/person was again mentioned in 15:6. His fate was that he was cast away and burned up with fire. This is obviously not a believer, of whom Jesus said He would not cast away (Jn. 6:38) and of whom the Bible never says would get burned. While their works may be burned with fire, they themselves are never imaged as being burned with fire.

So this was a person who seemed like he was a true believer, but was actually not. Jesus' point here is that the true believer was one who abides in Christ, which is testified to by his bearing of fruit (cf. Mt. 7:17-18). Here fruit is an obedient, Spirit produced lifestyle, which is said to be loving Christ (15:10).

Colossians 1:21-23

The book of Colossians was written by Paul to one of the churches he founded in Asia Minor. It was a sister epistle to the book of Ephesians, containing many of the same themes and topics. The first chapter of this epistle is one of the greatest texts on the nature, function and work of the Lord Jesus Christ.

After giving of thanks for the Colossian Christians (1:3-8) and a statement of prayer on their behalf (1:9-12), Paul began a lengthy discussion of the God-man, Jesus. Paul's discussion of Christ begins with Christ's work, and proceeds through His deity, His relationship to the created world, His preeminence in God's created order and in the church, His role in reconciliation the Father wanted to accomplish, ending with what He accomplished for the Christians of Colossae. It is this last point that Paul makes in His explanation of Christ, which focuses upon the believer's perseverance of abiding.

In 1:21, Paul indicated to the Colossians that even though they were in a state of being, "alienated and hostile in mind, *engaged* in evil deeds" something amazing happened to them. They were "reconciled" by Christ's sacrifice (cf. 1:22). This reconciliation was for the purpose of presenting to God, the Father, a "holy and blameless and beyond reproach" church (cf. Eph. 5:25-27).

To these statements Paul added an exception clause in the next verse (1:23). This exception identified circumstances that if true would invalidate what he has just stated regarding them. In other words, if what follows was not true of them, then neither was what precedes. Paul said, it will be known that you have actually been reconciled "if indeed you continue in the faith firmly established and steadfast, and not moved away from the hope of the gospel."

The exception clause was their continuing or remaining in the faith, that is, being a continuous part of the faith. The faith representing here the truth of Christianity, both in reference to correct Christian teaching and correct Christian living. This continuance in the faith was explained through a series of attributes.

They should be "firmly established." The idea here was that of a solid or sure foundation. A foundation that had been laid well and continued on in that state. It was stable. They should also be "steadfast."

To be steadfast refers to the idea of firmness in structure. The first term focused upon the founding of something, but this term looked at what was built upon that sure foundation. What is built upon it is a firm structure. It is settled. Further, they should be "not moved away from the hope of the gospel."

This statement should be seen as a summary of the two other terms. This type of person was one who would not constantly shift from place to place (cf. Eph. 4:14). From what was it they would not shift? Paul said from the "hope of the gospel."

Paul mentioned this hope earlier in 1:5, "the hope laid up for you in heaven, of which you previously heard in the word of truth, the gospel." The hope of the gospel was glorified life in heaven with Christ (cf. 1:13). This gospel Paul went on to indicate was proclaimed to all the world of which he was a minister.

Paul's point here is clear. Believers, those who have truly been reconciled, are those who consistently continue on in true Christian teaching and living, and by so doing evidence they are founded and stable, totally unmoved, in the gospel hope.

1 John 2:19

In the first epistle of John, John maps out for his readers what the outcome of true believing faith is. He wants his readers absolutely sure on whether they possess eternal life or not, for he says, "These things I have written to you who believe in the name of the Son of God, in order that you may know that you have eternal life" (1 Jn. 5:13). How might this eternal life be described? John does not leave his readers guessing. In 5:11-12 he tells them that eternal life is given to the believer in Jesus Christ, who is Himself that life. The possession of the Son is tantamount for the apostle. In demonstrating this truth throughout the book, John indicates that the believer is one who abides in Christ. A particularly good example of this is found in the ninth verse of the second chapter, in which John identifies a problematic group within the church that has been causing problems. Of them John says, "They went out from us, but they were not *really* of us; for if they had been of us, they would have remained with us; but *they went out*, in order that it might be shown that they all are not of us." To understand this statement the teaching and character of these people must be mentioned.

John indicates several things they were doing that were disturbing the churches, for which the apostle John was responsible. They were trying to deceive the community (2:26). They were also resistant to the apostolic witness and message (4:5-6). Further, they were claiming spiritual sources for their message (4:1-4, 6). John also gives some of their practices. These individuals were elitist and lofty in the practices and interactions with other believers (2:9-11; 3:17; 4:20-21). They were giving a message that sought to be popular (3:13; 4:5-6). In their teachings they were separating holiness and belief. Several of their beliefs were also mentioned in the epistle. These were: 1) special knowledge of God (2:3-6; 2:20-25, 27; 2) special illumination to get that knowledge (2:20-25, 27); 3) special way to eternal life (2:26); 4) they had a new teaching (2:7); and 5) Christ did not come in the flesh (4:2-3; 5:1-5).

For these reasons, John opens his letter with a strong statement of his apostolic authority. John and the other disciples were the eyewitnesses of Jesus life and message (1:1). He was manifested to them from the Father and they in return proclaimed Him, who is eternal life (1:2). They proclaimed Him so that the hearers would have fellowship with the apostles, since it was the apostles who had fellowship with God (1:3). John's point here was that fellowship with God could only be validated if the person claiming to have fellowship with God also had fellowship with the apostles.

This is what marked the church from the very beginning. Notice the words of Acts 2:41-42 as it recorded the acts of the first believer's after Peter's first sermon, "So then, those who had received his word were baptized; and there were added that day about three thousand souls. And they were continually devoting themselves to the apostles' teaching and to fellowship, to the breaking of bread and to prayer."

This group of people in 1 John chose to not remain properly related to the teachings and lifestyle of the apostles, and therefore John declared of them that, "they were not *really* of us." Abiding in Christian teaching and living is the mark of a true Christian. Not doing that evidences just the opposite.

Summary

So what might be said about the perseverance of the believer? First and foremost, the perseverance of the saints may rightly be said to be the perseverance by God. God carries the saint to his final destination. Hebrews 13:5 contains the promise of God that He will never leave us or forsake us. We can be completely confident in God completing His part of the task. The believer is to respond, though, to this working of God in his life. Paul says in Philippians 2:12-13, "So then, my beloved, just as you have always obeyed, not as in my presence only, but now much more in my absence, work out your salvation with fear and trembling." The believer constantly strives toward laying hold of that for which he was laid hold of by God (Phil. 3:12-16). The believer will not stay in perpetual ongoing sin with no change. The seed of God's salvation is in him which will ultimately bloom in heaven.

Conclusion

God's processes in salvation are therefore very clear. In eternity past God designed a plan whereby He might gain for Himself all the glory. He would redeem a certain number from a fallen race. That fallen race was man, who fell in the garden destroying the image of God in which he was created. This made man totally devoid of righteousness and totally affected by wickedness in all his parts.

God chose those whom He would redeem based on His own good pleasure. In order to redeem them He had to both make a way for their guilt and sin to be propitiated for and to provide a way to place them in a state which would be suitable to exist with Him. Such was done through the sacrifice of his only begotten Son, who was sent into the world at the fullness of time to redeem fallen man (Gal. 4:4-5).

This atonement made by Christ was for those whom God the Father had chosen to receive, although for the rest of mankind, it abated the wrath of God for a time. Once the plan of salvation had been designed, God irresistibly drew and draws the elect to His Son in order for them to be regenerated and believe.

Having received a new inner man and believed, they are then protected and kept by God for the ultimate completion of their redemption, their receiving of a new body, so they might dwell with Him forever. As God keeps them, they respond by keeping themselves in His love and in His teaching, manifested and witnessed to in the teaching of the apostles. In summary, this is the teaching of the doctrine of grace.

What better conclusion can be made to these great truths than what the apostle made regarding the purposes of God's elective grace, "And *he did so* in order that He might make known the riches of His glory upon vessels of mercy, which He prepared beforehand for glory, *even* us, whom He also called, not from among Jews only, but also from among the Gentiles" (Rom. 9:23-24).

What follows are two appendixes. The first is regarding the matter of Christian assurance and the second focuses upon the causes and mediums of salvation.

Appendix 1
The Christian's Confidence:
A Brief Discussion of Christian Assurance

I feel it necessary to take a few moments before you read this appendix to set its content within the broader context of the ministry of God taking place at Berean Bible Baptist Church, where I am the senior pastor. In a series on the Great Commission from 2006 to 2009, I had taken each facet of the commission and offered an extensive explanation of it, by examining the New Testament's teaching on that particular area. When we reached the point of the commission in which Jesus called the disciples to "make disciples," the congregation was challenged in some very intense ways.

While studying this important duty of the Christian, from such passages as Luke 9:57-62 and Matthew 16:24-27, several members of the flock identified their need for greater understanding in the area of Christian assurance. I believe this to be a normal response to true gospel preaching, which will be clear as you digest the content of this appendix. So I took a slight break from that series to comply with that request. This appendix was the result of answering that request. Thus, in a very real sense, this appendix has arisen out of a pastoral concern for the establishment of a truly biblical foundation for assurance. I have decided to leave much of the personal style within the written form of this appendix.

The relationship of this discussion to the study of the doctrines of grace cannot be underestimated. Peter identified the link between election and assurance when he made the following statement in 2 Peter 1:8-11, after recording a list of spiritual virtues to be pursued by believers,

> For if these qualities are yours and are increasing, they render you neither useless nor unfruitful in the true knowledge of our Lord Jesus Christ. For he who lacks these qualities is blind or short-sighted, having forgotten his purification from his former sins. Therefore, brethren, be all the more diligent to make certain about His calling and choosing you; for as long as you practice these things, you will never stumble; for in this way the entrance into the eternal kingdom of our Lord and Savior Jesus Christ will be abundantly supplied to you.

Assurance and election, two connected spiritual realities.

Objective

According to many of you, the last few messages I have preached here at Berean have been quite convicting and have lead many of you to engage in some serious introspection regarding your salvation and the salvation of some of your family members. While it has been my goal to re-establish the biblical discipline of introspection back into our modern religious climate that disregards it at best and rejects it at worst, even that discipline must be practiced within the proper biblical context. Introspection is not meant to lead to despair and hopelessness. Instead, it should eventually point us in the direction of true confidence and security, which is in Jesus Christ.

The Basis of Our Confidence

When it comes to the matter of the assurance of one's salvation there are four different senses upon which a healthy view of one's salvation ought to be constructed. Those four are the absolute, relative, subjective, and objective senses. All four of these play a role in providing the Christian with a biblically grounded perspective of their conversion.

The first is the absolute sense. By absolute, I mean that it is impossible for those who truly have been converted to lose their salvation and be condemned to hell. It is in this sense that the constitution of our church states that in Christ believers have "the divine guarantee that they shall never perish." We stand confidently on such a passage as John 10:28-29, which supports our belief in this regard. This is sometimes referred to as eternal security. Once a person is saved, he or she is eternally secure.

However, security can also be discussed in a relative sense. By relative sense, it is meant that our security hinges upon certain actions carried out in us in relationship to God. The concept of relative security is that believers, despite temporary failings and sins, are maintained by God as they cling to Christ and persevere in good deeds, as John 15:1-6 and Ephesians 2:10 teach us. If the absolute sense is best described as eternal security, then the relative sense is best described as perseverance of the saints.

A third sense in which to understand our security is the subjective sense. By subjective, I mean that true believers, by bringing forth fruit, manifest to themselves and to other believers that they are truly children of God. This is obviously related to the relative sense of security. Many passages teach just this very truth. Matthew 7:20 states, "So then, you will know them by their fruits." John 13:35 states, "By this all men will know that you are My disciples, if you have love for one another." John 15:8 states, "By this is My Father glorified, that you bear much fruit, and so prove to be My disciples."

Finally, the objective sense, which is related to the absolute sense, is the last of the senses in which our security can be understood. By objective sense, it is meant that by faith, a person has both followed through on the directions of the Word of God as to what one must do to be saved, and he or she trusts that God has responded to that faith as He has promised in His Word. The Bible tells us to repent and believe on Christ. Therefore, that is what we must do to be saved. All four of these senses will impact our sense of assurance. So, there are grounds on which people can have confidence that they truly do know Jesus as their Lord and Savior.

The Effort of Our Confidence

The next reality that I would like to note is that although God and Scripture provide assurance, it is nonetheless to be pursued and worked at by every Christian. When describing the matter of assurance, Peter made the following statement, "Therefore, brethren, be all the more diligent to make certain about His calling and choosing you; for as long as you practice these things, you will never stumble; for in this way the entrance into the eternal kingdom of our Lord and Savior Jesus Christ will be abundantly supplied to you" (2 Peter 1:10-11). Let me be very clear here. If you want a way to be comfortably made assure of your salvation, the Bible does not offer you such a solution. Assurance is the result of Christian effort, as is any other spiritual reality manifested in the Christian life. It is not entered into easily. Let me examine this idea more closely with you.

Peter indicated that the believer must be "diligent to make certain" in this effort of fully experiencing assurance. The idea of being diligent basically means to do something in a hurry or to make haste. Usually, when someone does something in a hurried manner, he or she does so because he or she has an eagerness to carry it out and is intense about it. Therefore, in Peter's day, this word could also be used to communicate the idea of being zealous or taking pains to do something. It is in fact this idea that is prominent in Peter's statement.

Notice that the diligence spoken of in this passage is a conclusion, which the conjunction "Therefore" indicates. This fact points the believer to the reality that vigorously pursuing the evidence of fruitfulness, which is the subject matter of the previous verses, is the best way to gain assurance. There are a couple of implications of this pursuit. The first one is that "you will never stumble." In other words, you will have a more consistent Christian life. Another impact is that the kingdom will be "abundantly supplied to you," which speaks of a greater assurance of your salvation and an expectation of future approval by Christ.

The Past/Present/Future and Our Confidence

Saints, it is intriguing to me that the Bible rarely points the believer to the past when it comes to the matter of salvation. Even when it does point the believer to the past, it is normally to motivate the believer to greater or more consistent Christian behavior in the present. In other words, the basis of assurance is not the past but the present. Why? The reason is that for the Christian, the experience of salvation is always in the now. One thing we must understand though, is that the basis of salvation is in the past, because the basis of salvation is what Christ did on the cross. However, regarding your personal experience of salvation and assurance, the present moment is what is critical.

So when I consider the past, it is not so that I might sit comfortably and smug about my salvation. Instead, it is so that I might be more motivated to pursue the life God has chosen me to experience. In other words, even when my past salvation experience is mentioned, the Bible does so for present reasons. Listen to Peter again, "Since you have in obedience to the truth purified your souls for a sincere love of the brethren, fervently love one another from the heart, for you have been born again not of seed which is perishable but imperishable, that is, through the living and abiding word of God" (1 Peter 1:22-23). Do you see how Peter appealed to the past in order to motivate the believers to whom he wrote in the present?

This means that when I am considering my assurance, it is not enough to only consider the question, "Have I received Christ as Lord in the past?" Just as critical, and even more so, is the question, "Am I willing to live with Him as Lord today?" In other words, "Am I willing to choose Him again today?" It is not only, "Did I exercise faith in Christ as an eight year old, but also am I living by faith in Christ at this particular time?" Nor is it simply whether I became a Christian and owned Christ in college, but also, "Do I own Christ now in my work place and with my new friends who are not aware of my Christian faith?"

The experience of salvation is not just a past tense issue. It is both a present tense and a future tense issue as well. However, I am not experiencing either the past or the future right now (at least not in a full sense), but I am walking in the present. Therefore, when it comes to the matter of the assurance on one's salvation, the present is the critical part of the equation. Even when the past and the future are considered, they are considered regarding their impact on me now. It is these issues that can quite easily lead to self-deception. Let us consider this reality.

The Reality of False Confidence

We can become so confident in the way that we see the past that nothing in our present can convince us that our past experience was simply religious emotionalism, religious awareness, or human-produced religious reformation instead of the true religious conversion that the Scriptures advocate. The Bible never meant for this to be the case. This is a very dangerous state in which to be, because in effect we disown our present.

This does not make sense, because the present is the very tense in which the validity of our religious experience is most lived. It is our present that tells the validity of our past religious experience. One of the primary reasons that this takes place is because people tend to absolutize the Christian life in all of its given facets and perspectives. In other words, they tend to make the absolute aspect of salvation the only aspect of salvation. As long as you said this prayer, or raised your hand, you are in. They do not care how you live after that.

This can be particularly troublesome in trying to make sense of our Christian lives. I find this to be the case when considering the salvation of children. You see, eternal security is built not on profession, but on possession.

The Fact of It

Something that has become quite common here at Berean is the practice of adults being baptized, although they had been baptized as children. The essential reason for this is that they have become convinced through honest evaluation of their lives, understanding, decisions, and commitment that they were not saved as children, although many around them assumed they were. The reasons differ from person to person.

Some were simply pushed forward by eager parents, who wanted to get the salvation issue out of the way without really examining their child's profession. Others followed the decisions of other people, and convinced themselves that they had made a similar decision, too. Still, others were moved by something they heard in a sermon and made a decision that was not based on the gospel but on the emotional upheavals through which they were going. It is important to remember that, according to the word of Jesus, there is a reception of the gospel marked by joy that falls short of true conversion. It falls short, because it is temporary (Matthew 13:20-22). It is produced by an inflamed emotional condition, which does not endure the test of having to stand upon the Word of God against the world and its delights.

Whatever the case was, any baptism such an individual experienced was little more than wetting of the skin and was far from what Jesus demanded. Jesus demanded what we refer to as believer's baptism or creedal baptism. Those terms mean that the individual being baptized based the baptism upon an actual confession of the Lord Jesus Christ. Those choosing to be re-baptized for this reason have chosen the right pathway.

The Basis of It

The question we need to answer is, "Why does this type of self-deception take place?" Well, the basic reason behind this reality is found in the quagmire known as the human heart. According to Jeremiah 17:9, "The heart is more deceitful than all else And is desperately sick; Who can understand it?" So there is a basic problem with our core that leads to self-deception and misunderstanding in the spiritual realm. Therefore, false profession is an issue with which the church must deal.

However, this does not mean that a child cannot be saved. We wholeheartedly believe in the conversion of children and thus, their need to hear the gospel proclaimed to them, also. The last statement is important, because although we believe in the conversion of children, we do not believe that they are converted in a sense that is different from how an adult is converted. Let me explain.

The Safeguard Against It

In Genesis 15:1-6, God set the pattern of how a person was to be saved. The pattern was that by grace through faith the sinner would be reckoned to be righteous, which speaks of being justified (cf. Romans 4). This has always been the one and only method by which salvation takes place, and it always will be. While it was defined in progressively more detailed fashion throughout the revelation of God, in holy Scripture it was never changed.

Therefore, since an adult must receive salvation by grace, then a child must receive it by grace, also. Since adults must deny themselves, take up their crosses, and follow Christ, then children must do the same. There is no junior method of salvation by which God allows children to skip any of the objective steps to conversion and get in through an abbreviated method.

We must be careful that we know what we mean when we say that children can be saved. Yes, they can be saved, but they must be saved by the same means as any other person is saved. Clearly, Jesus believed this to be the case, because when it came to the matter of describing how one received the kingdom, He used a child as the example of such (Mark 10:13-16; cf. Matthew 18:1-3).

It is at this point that some will raise an objection by indicating that a child does not have the ability to understand the truths of the Christian faith like an adult does. I agree wholeheartedly with this assessment. However, my response to that is this: given that to be true, can such a child who does not understand the truths of the Christian faith thus be saved?

In other words, can the failure to understand that one is a sinner who will surely be punished in the lake of fire for their sins be acceptable in pronouncing a person saved? What else can they not understand and still be considered saved? Can they fail to understand that Jesus is God and was raised from the dead and still be considered saved?

To pronounce that a person can fail to understand the truths of Christianity and still be saved is to say that there is an alternate way to heaven other than the gospel. The issue is this: Is the gospel and understanding its message required for conversion or is it not? If it is, then it is. If it is not, then it is not. You cannot have it both ways, with some people needing the gospel and others not needing it. That is impossible! What is true of Jesus is true of the gospel that bears Him to the world, "And there is salvation in no one else; for there is no other name under heaven that has been given among men, by which we must be saved (Acts 4:12).

However, I would be in error if I did not recognize that there is a maturing, or growth, that takes place in a converted person's understanding. Also, it is that growth and the person's response to it that can tell whether a person is actually saved. Growth in one's thinking is an assumed fact of human existence.

It is for that reason that Paul could write the following in 1 Corinthians 13:11, "When I was a child, I used to speak as a child, think as a child, reason as a child; when I became a man, I did away with childish things." Therefore, it is no surprise that in this same letter Paul calls the Corinthians to mature in their thinking or their reasoning about spiritual matters. We see this in 1 Corinthians 14:20: "Brethren, do not be children in your thinking; yet in evil be babes, but in your thinking be mature."

This stands behind many of the apostle's prayers for the saints. For example, part of what he wrote to the Colossians regarding his prayer for them is, "For this reason also, since the day we heard of it, we have not ceased to pray for you and to ask that you may be filled with the knowledge of His will in all spiritual wisdom and understanding, so that you may walk in a manner worthy of the Lord, to please Him in all respects, bearing fruit in every good work and increasing in the knowledge of God" (Colossians 1:9-10). Notice that he prayed for them to "be filled with the knowledge of His will in all spiritual wisdom and understanding." Does he mean that they had no knowledge of God's will in those areas?

He definitely did not mean that. They could not have been Christians without some level of knowledge. Therefore, his focus must be upon them increasing in these matters. This becomes clear when we read verse 10, where we see that he prayed that they would increase "in the knowledge of God."

The author of Hebrews linked his audience's failure to understand what he wanted to say about Melchizedek to their lack of spiritual maturity. Therefore, he wrote, "Concerning him we have much to say, and it is hard to explain, since you have become dull of hearing. For though by this time you ought to be teachers, you have need again for someone to teach you the elementary principles of the oracles of God, and you have come to need milk and not solid food" (Hebrews 5:11-12).

Obviously, he is dealing on the level of spiritual knowledge and understanding, which is just as important as spiritual behavior and actions. This is validated when he remarked in Hebrews 6:1-3, "Therefore, leaving the elementary teaching about the Christ, let us press on to maturity, not laying again a foundation of repentance from dead works and of faith toward God, of instruction about washings, and laying on of hands, and the resurrection of the dead, and eternal judgment. And this we shall do, if God permits." Clearly, he has in mind, not just maturing in behavior, but also maturing in thinking and understanding.

Something else is important here, however. Notice how the author of Hebrews introduces us to a critical part of this growth in one's thinking: "And this we shall do, if God permits" (Hebrews 6:3). It is the sovereign working of God in the person's life that allows for this maturing in one's thinking to take place. This is why growth in the grasping of spiritual matters and their significance is one of the signs of true conversion. It witnesses to God's workings in that person's life (cf. Philippians 2:12-13).

Since the growth is tied to God's sovereign workings, it will also be accompanied by a submission to God's sovereign means. In other words, as we often say here at Berean, God ordains the means, as well as the end. If the end towards which God works is mature spiritual thinking, then God will also prescribe the means. The Bible identifies the means as the teaching by God's gifted teachers. Therefore, there must be submissiveness to the teaching process, because the process of being spiritually guided and directed marks the truly converted heart.

Well did James remark, "This you know, my beloved brethren. But let everyone be quick to hear, slow to speak and slow to anger; for the anger of man does not achieve the righteousness of God" (James 1:19-20). Peter also remarked well when he wrote, "Therefore, putting aside all malice and all guile and hypocrisy and envy and all slander, like newborn babes, long for the pure milk of the word, that by it you may grow in respect to salvation, if you have tasted the kindness of the Lord" (1 Peter 2:1-3).

We have established the fact that, within believers, there is a growth in their understanding of spiritual truth. We have also seen that such a growth is potentially one of the markers of true conversion. Therefore, we can with confidence state that a child will have a rudimentary grasp of the spiritual matters that stand behind the gospel. Also, those children who are truly saved will grow in their grasp of these things. So we can say that, although a child will not understand them at the level of a spiritually mature adult, the child will understand and grasp them at a spiritual child's level. In other words, as children come to know more of the matters that define Christianity, they will respond in clearly spiritual fashion if they are truly saved.

Let me illustrate this. A nine or ten year old boy might understand that to deny himself, take up his cross, and follow Christ would demand a change from him always wanting things to go his way. Then as the child becomes a teenager or young adult, he would more fully grasp that it also means that he must further reject the enticements of the world and his peers to live according to the spirit of this age. While an adult would grasp both of these matters simultaneously, a child would grow in his or her comprehension. What a child does with this further knowledge would demonstrate whether he or she was truly saved.

Quite frankly, this is where the rubber meets the road for many church kids. They seem to show signs of conversion when they are young and in Sunday school and Junior church. They love to read their Bibles and sing the songs of the church. But as a child begins to age and the demands of Christ become clearer, a decision needs to be made again. It is not that he or she gets saved again. What I mean is that the earlier decision must be affirmed, almost in the sense of being ratified. However, this is not limited to children who grow up in the church. Anyone who makes a confession may make that confession on less than actual experience. Let me show this first in the biblical text then try to illustrate it. Turn to John 6.

It is in this chapter that the great Bread of Life declaration is made by Christ in reference to Himself. He fed the five thousand, and many of those who were fed tracked Him down the next day to get more. They did not want more of His teaching, but more of His bread. To them, it was time to eat again.

Jesus knew their feigned commitment to Him was simply built upon the fact that they ate. The text says, "Jesus answered them and said, 'Truly, truly, I say to you, you seek Me, not because you saw signs, but because you ate of the loaves, and were filled'" (John 6:26). This lead to a prolonged dialogue between the crowd and Jesus in which He affirmed that their commitment to Him was not authentic. He said that was the case essentially because they were not given to Him by the Father and had not been drawn to Him and taught of the Father (John 6:35-37, 44-45). Jesus then dropped on them His most controversial statement to date, which was that to have life, one had to eat His flesh and drink His blood. In other words, only by committing oneself completely to Him and receiving Him could one have life (John 6:46-58).

This statement was so controversial that it led to two different responses among His followers, those who had been separated from the multitudes to be His disciples. One response was recorded by John as follows, "Many therefore of His disciples, when they heard this said, 'This is a difficult statement; who can listen to it'" (John 6:60)? This led to what is written in John 6:66, "As a result of this many of His disciples withdrew, and were not walking with Him anymore." When their understanding of the Christian faith became clearer they evidenced that they were not truly converted; they were unwilling to respond to the greater understanding in a distinctively converted manner. However, notice the other response.

Right after John recorded the leaving of many of Christ's previously faithful followers, it says, "Jesus said therefore to the twelve, 'You do not want to go away also, do you'" (John 6:67)? Now notice the dialogue that ensues, "Simon Peter answered Him, 'Lord, to whom shall we go? You have the words of eternal life. And we have believed and have come to know that You are the Holy One of God.' Jesus answered them, 'Did I Myself not choose you, the twelve, and yet one of you is a devil'" (John 6:68-70).

In this passage we see two sets of people who were thought to be at one time just one group. In other words, they were all thought to be true believers and followers of Christ. At one time, all of these people seemed to have responded positively to the message of Jesus Christ. However, when Christ's message eventually became clearer and more demanding, it was manifested that this one group was actually comprised of two very different groups. One of those groups was saved and the other group was not. What is my point?

Quite simply, when true believers find out the depth of the demands of following Christ, they choose again to deny themselves, take up their crosses, and follow Him, just as they had truly done earlier. However, as the other group hears and understands the demands, the fact that they had never truly chosen to follow Christ in the first place manifests itself, and they turn away. Sometimes it is not immediate, but it will eventually show (cf. 1 John 2:18-19). Oftentimes, they first turn away in their behavior and then finally in their presence; they abandon church and the things of God completely. The abandonment of the church was the final step in a series of distancing actions and attitudes, which were mini-abandonments, which had already taken place.

The Conclusion

So what is the ultimate point that we must understand from these things? Saints, first and foremost, we must recognize that introspection is biblical. However, not only is it biblical, but based on our study, it must be conducted in a biblical fashion. Listen to the words of the apostle Paul in a passage to which we have often referred, "Test yourselves to see if you are in the faith; examine yourselves! Or do you not recognize this about yourselves, that Jesus Christ is in you – unless you fail the test" (2 Corinthians 13:5).

Within this statement of the apostle Paul, we see three key ideas of which we should make note, given our subject matter. First, this statement alone is sufficient to alert modern American Christianity to the fact that the Christian faith without the practice of holy introspection is not Christianity at all. Paul calls for the Corinthians to put themselves to the test, which means to be engaged in self-examination. Would he do anything less to any other group of believers? Are we better than the Corinthians were? I think not.

Next, take note of what Paul said was to be tested, "if you are in the faith." Here, the idea of "the faith" is that of the "Way" that we see throughout the book of Acts (cf. Acts 9:2; 19:9, 23; 22:4; 24:14, 22). This is Christianity in its broadest terms, including not just Christian doctrine and Christian behavior, but the whole Christian existence in all of its facets. The test is not of maturity, but rather of possession over and against profession. This point was validated when Paul references the purpose for the test, which was "that Jesus Christ is in you." You are testing to validate possession beyond just naked profession.

Finally, note here that Paul holds out the possibility that a person could have attached themselves to a local church and been functioning as a Christian in that church, but not really be one. After all, he stated, "unless you fail the test." So, introspection is biblical.

Not only is introspection biblical, it must be carried out biblically. An example of these two issues lays behind the words of Jesus to the seven churches of Asia Minor, to whom the book of Revelation was written. To each of the seven churches, Jesus had a specific word, either of commendation or rebuke. Some of the churches, in fact most of the churches, received a combination message of both commendation and rebuke. Let me illustrate this from the first example, the church of Ephesus.

> To the angel of the church in Ephesus write: The One who holds the seven stars in His right hand, the

> One who walks among the seven golden lampstands, says this: I know your deeds and your toil and perseverance, and that you cannot endure evil men, and you put to the test those who call themselves apostles, and they are not, and you found them to be false; and you have perseverance and have endured for My name's sake, and have not grown weary. But I have this against you, that you have left your first love. Remember therefore from where you have fallen, and repent and do the deeds you did at first; or else I am coming to you, and will remove your lampstand out of its place – unless you repent. Yet this you do have, that you hate the deeds of the Nicolaitans, which I also hate. He who has an ear, let him hear what the Spirit says to the churches. To him who overcomes, I will grant to eat of the tree of life, which is in the Paradise of God (Revelation 2:1-7).

Why are these words of Christ necessary? For the most part, these churches had not engaged in self-examination and had continued down pathways that called into question the validity of their ultimate commitments to Christ. For this reason, Christ calls them out and beckons them to make adjustment that only genuine believers could make. Although they had not examined themselves, He had examined them and come to certain conclusions. In a sense, He was calling them to self-examination to see what He saw and to respond appropriately. What are the things that led Christ to the responses recorded here?

The first example we see in the church of Ephesus is that of a waning, or regression, in holy affections: "But I have this against you, that you left your first love" (Revelation 2:4). Although they were a shining example of religious service and behavior, a passion for the Savior and the things of the Savior were no longer there. Another example of an area of examination was that of adopting false teaching. To the church of Pergamum He noted, "But I have a few things against you, because you have there some who hold the teaching of Balaam, who kept teaching Balak to put a stumbling block before the sons of Israel, to eat things sacrificed to idols, and to commit acts of immorality" (Revelation 2:14). Believers in their midst were holding to teachings that contradicted the true Christian faith.

A third cause of rebuke by Christ was the lack of discipline within the church. In other words, they were accommodating the religiously defiant. John was told to write to Thyatira, "But I have this against you, that you tolerate the woman Jezebel, who calls herself a prophetess, and she teaches and leads My bond-servants astray, so that they commit acts of immorality and eat things sacrificed to idols" (Revelation 2:20). Another case of rebuke is based on the lack of zealous pursuit of righteousness. We see this when Christ tells the church of Sardis, "Wake up, and strengthen the things that remain, which were about to die; for I have not found your deeds completed in the sight of My God" (Revelation 3:2).

So we see four critical, biblically based areas of self-examination on which a believer can concentrate in order to evaluate whether or not he is evidencing those realities that confirm the decision he believes he made in the past. Again, those areas are holy affections, teaching, relationships, and practical righteousness. In reference to holy affections, I should consider whether my desires for God and love of God have increased as I have grown in my understanding of who God is and what He does. I should ask, "Do I accept God for who He says He is and love Him?" Also, I should ask, "Do I love the things that God loves, or does the love of the world always trump loving God and what matters to God?"

In reference to the matter of teaching, I should consider whether I easily get caught up in what I find out later to be false teaching. Also, I should evaluate whether there is an ever increasing desire within me for biblical instruction, not just on issues with which I am dealing, but with anything having to do with the things of the Lord. Further, the true believer submits not just to the Word of God, but also to the one who bears it to him or her. That being the case, I should also consider whether I am truly submissive to my spiritual leaders who give me instruction and seek to edify me in the faith.

Next, let us consider the issue of relationships. One of the areas of concern here would be whether I desire and pursue fellowship with the people of God. I should ask things such as, "Am I practicing, in greater fashion, those spiritual disciplines that foster good relationships, such as forbearance, forgiveness, humility, kindness, gentleness, etc. Do I possess a longing to be where the people of God are, which is at church, or is missing church an insignificant issue to me?" Also, critical here is for me to consider whether I am refusing to foster intimate friendships with those who practice ungodly behavior, without a clear evangelistic intention and plan for reaching them. In other words, do I own Christ before others who do not know Him, and am I making Him a part of the conversation and interaction? Around unbelievers, do I act as if I am an unbeliever, or do I appear religiously neutral? These are all clues as to whether I am truly converted.

The fourth area in which I can and ought to examine myself is that of practical righteousness. I should consider whether my obedience to Christ's demands have grown in depth and extent. I would also evaluate whether I respond to personal sin in a biblical fashion, by repenting from known sins and pursuing a pathway of victory over them that is marked by Scriptural principles and methods. I should ask, "Does sin concern me more or less than it used to? Have particular sinful holds in my life gained more victory over me than I have gained over them?"

These are some of the steps that the believer can and must take to evaluate, or examine his standing before God. Were you saved as a child? Do you wonder at the genuine nature of your conversion? Examine yourself in a biblical fashion. Do you commit yourself again to follow Christ when you learn more about Him and His demands? Or in your heart, do you turn away from His demands in favor of the world's demands? Are you drawn away from Christ and put up no resistance? Or do you find yourself irresistibly drawn to the Savior in spite of what you now know and what it means for you? Are spiritual disciplines becoming increasingly important to you or less important? As we test ourselves, we should also remember that Christ is the answer to everything that might surface in this test.

Even if it surfaces that we are not saved, we should remember the words of Jesus to the church of Laodicea, who had failed the test of conversion for the most part. He said, "Behold, I stand at the door and knock; if anyone hears My voice and opens the door, I will come in to him, and will dine with him, and he with Me" (Revelation 3:20). Christ is always there to accept the repentant sinner.

Appendix 2

Causes of Salvation

The *Original Cause* is the sovereign will of God, for nothing can come into being save that which He decreed before the foundation of the world.

The *Meritorious Cause* is the mediatorial work of Christ, who "obtained eternal redemption" (Heb. 9:22) for His people, purchasing for them all the blessings of it by His perfect obedience to the Law and His sacrificial death.

The *Efficient Cause* is the varied operations of the Holy Spirit, who applies to the elect the benefits purchased by Christ, capacitating them to enjoy the same and making them meet for the inheritance of the saints in light.

The *Ministerial Cause* and means is the preaching of the Word (James 1:21), because it discovers to us where salvation is to be obtained.

The *Instrumental Cause* is faith, by which the sinner receives or comes into possession of and obtains an interest in Christ and His redemption.

Such distinctions as these are not merely technicalities for theologians, but are part of the faith once delivered unto the saints, and unless they apprehend the same they are liable to be deceived by any Scripture-quoting false prophet who accosts them.

A. W. Pink, Sermon on the Mount

Appendix 3

Medium of Salvation

In discussing the medium of salvation, the concern is identifying that process through which an unbeliever becomes a believer. The divine persons are not in view [ex. we are saved by the Holy Spirit (1 Peter 1:2)], but rather those things used by the divine persons in order to accomplish their goal of salvation. There are several terms that are used to explain how one moves from darkness unto life. These terms are election, common grace, general call, effectual call, regeneration, faith, conversion, justification, sanctification, perseverance of the saints, and glorification. Each of these terms will be succinctly expounded.

Election (John 6; Romans 9; Ephesians 1; 1 Peter 1)

Election is that act of God whereby He sets aside by efficacious decree before the creation of the world a specific number from amongst the masses of hell bound men to be benefactors of His special act of salvation.

Common Grace (John 14, 16; 2 Thessalonians 2)

Common grace is that working of the Holy Spirit in the world at large, which is short of regeneration, that restrains evil, allows for civil good, delays the judgment of God, and convicts of sin, righteousness and judgment.

General Call (Romans 10)

General call is that gracious invitation to receive the benefits of the salvation affected by Christ that is offered to all men, but although not always effectual, is still a genuine call. This call demonstrates God's righteous standard, and His love for sinners, and results in further condemnation for those who reject it, and salvation for those who except it.

Effectual Call (John 6; Romans 8)

The effectual call is that act of God whereby He definitively draws and regenerates those whom He has elected for salvation.

Regeneration (Romans 11; 1 Thessalonians 1)

Regeneration is that act of God whereby He changes the will of the sinner so that it now chooses that which it naturally resists, the good, and implants new life in them, with the result that he becomes a believer.

Faith (Ephesians 2)

Faith is that act of man whereby he claims for himself the new life and other benefits of Christ's atonement for himself, casting himself completely and wholly upon Christ for his eternal salvation, and it is a gift of God.

Conversion (1 Thessalonians 1)

Conversion is that act of man whereby he turns from his own self willed way of sin and embraces the Savior as his own.

Justification (Romans 3-7)

Justification is that act of God whereby he pronounces the regenerated sinner righteous in His sight. It is positional in nature.

Sanctification (Romans 6-8; Galatians 3-6)

Sanctification is that act of God whereby He progressively makes the regenerated sinner righteous, which is a continual process while he is in a non-glorified state, and to which the believer responds with obedience and love of Christ, which is positional, progressive, and prospective (future).

Perseverance (Romans 8; Philippians 2)

Perseverance of the saints is that continued act of the Holy Spirit in the believer's life whereby what God has begun in the believer's life is continued until the time of its completion, thereby assuring that none of God's elect are ultimately lost.

Glorification (1 Corinthians 15; 1 John 3)

Glorification is that act of God whereby He resurrects or translates the believer from this earthly body into a heavenly body, made after the form of Christ.

This is the process whereby God brings about the salvation of man. It will be noticed that it begins in eternity past with God, is activated in the present through God, and is completed in the future by God. Salvation is a work of God, with which man has the joyous privilege of participation.

Notes

1. Hodge, C. (1997). *Systematic Theology*. Originally published 1872. (electronic ed.) (1:1). Oak Harbor WA: Logos Research Systems, Vol. 1, 543.

2. Elwell, *Evangelical*, 81; J. C. O'Neil, "Arminianism" in *The Westminister Dictionary of Christian Theology*, Alan Richardson and John Bowden, eds. (Philadelphia: The Westminister Press, 1983), 43.

3. John H. Leith, An Introduction to the Reformed Tradition, Rev. Ed. (Atlanta: John Knox Press, 1981), 38.

4. Justo L. Gonzalez, *The Story of Christianity*, 2 vols., *The Reformation to the Present Day*, vol. 2 (San Francisco: Harper & Row, Publishers, 1985), 2:179.

5. Ibid.

6. J. C. O'Neil, 43.

7. It should be noted that Francis Gomarus followed closely the teachings of predestination as formulated by Theodore Beza, Calvin's successor in Geneva.

8. Gonzalez, *The Story*, 2:180.

9. F. L. Cross and E. A. Livingstone, "Arminianism," in *The Oxford Dictionary of The Christian Church*, 2nd ed. (New York: Oxford University Press, 1974), 90.

10. Elwell, *Evangelical*, 933.

11. Ibid., 332.

12. Ibid., 331-332

13. Ibid., 332.

14. Gonzalez, *The Story*, 182.

15. J. C. O'Neil, 43.

16. Paraclete being the Greek term used by John in recording Jesus' declaration regarding the Holy Spirit in John 14:16, translated "Helper."

17. Packer, J. I. *Concise Theology: A Guide to Historic Christian Beliefs*. (Tyndale House Publishers, 1993), 155.

18. Packer, *Concise Theology*, 131.

www.ingramcontent.com/pod-product-compliance
Lightning Source LLC
Chambersburg PA
CBHW020934090426
42736CB00010B/1130